UNMASKING

ISIS

THE

SHOCKING

TRUTH

ProgRESSive

2016

Unmasking ISIS
The Shocking Truth

© 2016 All rights reserved
ProgressivePress.com, San Diego, Calif.
Length: 48,000 words.
Paperback List Price: $13.95.
ISBN: 1-61577-164-6, EAN: 978-1-61577-164-6
Publication Date: April 4, 2016
E-book ISBN 1-61577-165-4
E-book Price $6.99

Co-author credits:

 "Unmasking ISIS" by George Washington's Blog
"Born of the USA" and further articles by Wayne Madsen
"The Brussels Bombings" by John-Paul Leonard

Library of Congress Subject Heading
ISIS/Daesh, LC: HV6433.I722

BISAC Subject Area Codes
POL037000 POLITICAL SCIENCE / Terrorism
POL036000 POLITICAL SCIENCE / Intelligence & Espionage
POL061000 POLITICAL SCIENCE / Genocide & War Crimes
POL045000 POLITICAL SCIENCE / Colonialism & Post-Colonialism
HIS027170 HISTORY / Military / Iraq War (2003-2011)
SOC058000 / POL506000 Conspiracy Investigations

ISIS started as rebels under the US occupation of Iraq, and grew by ravaging Libya and Syria. They fight as proxies for US neocons and their allies, who back them covertly via Saudi Arabia and Turkey. The motives are oil, gas, Africa's mineral wealth, and empire-building...

TABLE OF CONTENTS

Unmasking ISIS

by George Washington's Blog

Introduction

Where did ISIS come from? How was it able to gain land, arms and money so quickly?

This book will answer those questions ... and unmask ISIS.

Part 1 shows that the U.S. – through bad policies and stupid choices – is largely responsible for the rise of ISIS.

Part 2 reveals the strange history of the leaders of ISIS ... Including one who never really existed, and another who – if you read mainstream media drivel – was killed ... then arrested ... and then killed *again*.

Part 3 delves into the little-known, secret history of Iraq and Syria ... and discusses the *real* motivations behind our current policies towards those countries.

And Part 4 reveals the shocking truth about who is really supporting ISIS.

So grab a cup of coffee, and prepare to learn the *real* story.

Part 1: Oops … We Created a Monster

President Barack Obama noted[1] in an interview in March 2015:

ISIL [also known as ISIS] is a direct outgrowth of Al-Qaeda in Iraq that grew out of our invasion. Which is an example of unintended consequences. Which is why we should generally aim before we shoot.

He's correct. After all:

ISIS leaders *themselves* credit[2] the Iraq war for their success

- The New Yorker reports[3]: "ISIS is run by a council of former Iraqi generals …. Many are members of Saddam Hussein's secular Baath Party who converted to radical Islam in American prisons."

- Torture of Iraqis by Americans led to the rise of ISIS[4] … and America's Guantanamo prison inspired ISIS atrocities5

- Al Qaeda *wasn't* even *in* Iraq[6] until the U.S. invaded that country, as admitted[7] by President George W. Bush to ABC News in 2008:

  Bush: One of the major theaters against al Qaeda turns out to have been Iraq. This is where al Qaeda said they were going to take their stand. This is where al Qaeda was hoping to take …

  ABC News Interviewer: **But not until after the U.S. invaded.**

  Bush: Yeah, **that's right**. So what?

- ISIS took over large swaths of Iraq using captured American weapons left over from the Iraq war[8]

In addition, the entire American policy of arming "moderate" Syrian rebels has backfired.

Lebanon's Daily Star reports9 that so-called "moderate" Syrian rebels support ISIS terrorists:

"**We are collaborating with the Islamic State** and the Nusra Front [another extremist and hard-line Islamic terrorist group][10] by attacking the Syrian Army's gatherings in … Qalamoun," said Bassel Idriss, the **commander of an FSA-aligned rebel brigade**...

"**A very large number of FSA members have joined ISIS** and Nusra," Abu Fidaa [a retired Colonel in the Syrian army who is now the head of the Revolutionary Council in Qalamoun] said.

The so-called "moderate" Free Syrian Army has also signed a non-aggression pact[11] with ISIS[12].

The New York Times writes[13]:

President Obama's determination to train Syrian rebels to serve as ground troops against the Islamic State in Iraq and Syria leaves the United States dependent on a diverse group riven by infighting, with no shared leadership and with **hard-line Islamists as its most effective fighters**.

After more than three years of civil war, there are hundreds of militias fighting President Bashar al-Assad — and one another. Among them, **even the more secular forces have turned to Islamists for support and weapons** over the years, and **the remaining moderate rebels often fight alongside extremists** like the Nusra Front, Al Qaeda's affiliate in Syria...

Analysts who track the rebel movement say that **the concept of the Free Syrian Army as a unified force with an effective command structure is a myth**...

The Syrian rebels are a scattered archipelago of mostly local forces with ideologies that range from nationalist to jihadist. Their rank-and-file fighters are largely from the rural underclass, with **few having clear political visions beyond a general interest in** greater rights or **the dream of an Islamic state**...

Some European allies remain skeptical about the efficacy of arming the Syrian rebels. Germany, for instance, has been arming and training Kurdish pesh merga forces in Iraq, but has resisted doing the same for any groups in Syria — partly out of **fear that the weapons could end up in the hands of ISIS** or other radical groups.

"We can't really control the final destination of these arms," said Peter Wittig, the German ambassador to the United States...

The fluidity of battlefield alliances in Syria means that **even mainline rebels often end up fighting alongside the Nusra Front, whose suicide bombers are relied on by other groups** to soften up government targets.

"Even the groups that the U.S. has trained tend to show up in the same trenches as the Nusra Front **eventually, because they need them and they are fighting the same battles," Mr. Lund said...**

Current and former American officials acknowledge the government's lack of deep knowledge about the rebels. **"We need to do everything we can to figure out who the non-ISIS opposition is," said Ryan C. Crocker, a former United States ambassador to Iraq and Syria.** "Frankly, we don't have a clue."

And yet, as the Wall Street Journal[14], PBS[15], CNN[16], New York Times[17], Medium[18], Pulitzer prize-winning reporter Seymour Hersh[19] and others note, the U.S. and its allies have poured huge amounts of weapons and support to the Syrian Islamic "rebels". This is in *spite* of the CIA warning President Obama that arming rebels rarely works[20].

Washington wants regime change in Syria, so it's making up a myth of the "moderate Syrian rebel" who hates Assad and ISIS. But they "don't have a clue" as to whether such a mythical unicorn actually exists (spoiler alert: it doesn't).

The New York Times reported[21] in 2013 that *virtually all* of the rebel fighters in Syria are *hardline Islamic terrorists*. Things have gotten much worse since then ... as the few remaining moderates have been lured away by ISIS' arms, cash and influence.

Michael Shank – Adjunct Faculty and Board Member at George Mason University's School for Conflict Analysis and Resolution, and director of foreign policy at the Friends Committee on National Legislation – warned[22] a year ago:

> The Senate and House Intelligence committees' about-face decision last week[23] to arm the rebels in Syria is dangerous and disconcerting. **The weapons will assuredly end up in the wrong hands** and will only escalate the slaughter in Syria. Regardless of the vetting procedures in place, the sheer factionalized nature of the opposition guarantees that the arms will end up in some unsavory hands. The same militant fighters who have committed gross atrocities are among the best-positioned of the rebel groups to seize the weapons that the United States sends to Syria...

> Arming one side of Syria's multi-sided and bloody civil war **will come back to haunt us**. Past decisions by the U.S. to arm insurgencies in Libya, Angola, Central America and Afghanistan helped sustain brutal conflicts in those regions for decades. In the case of Afghanistan, arming the mujahideen in the 1980s created the instability that emboldened extreme militant groups and gave rise to the Taliban, which ultimately created an environment for al Qaeda to thrive...

> Arming the enemies of our enemies hasn't made the U.S. more friends; it has made the U.S. more enemies...

> Some armed opposition factions, including powerful Islamist coalitions, reject negotiation altogether[24]. Yet these are the same groups that will **likely seize control of U.S.-supplied weapons, just as they've already seized control of the bulk of the rebels' weaponry**...

> When you lift the curtain on the armed groups with the most formidable military presence on the ground in Syria, you find the Al Nusra Front and Al Farough Brigades. Both groups are closely aligned with Al Qaeda and have directly perpetrated barbaric atrocities. The Al Nusra Front has been charged with **beheadings** of civilians, while a commander from the Al Farough Brigades reportedly ate the heart of a pro-Assad soldier.

Shank's warning was ignored, and his worst fears came to pass. And since the Obama administration is doubling-down on the same moronic policy, it will happen again ...

And it's not as if we only started supporting the rebels after the Syrian civil war started. Rather, the U.S. started funding the Syrian opposition 5 years *before* the civil war started ... and started arming them 4 years beforehand[25].

And a leaked 2006 U.S. State Department Cable from the U.S. Ambassador to Syria discussed[26] plans to overthrow the Syrian government.

So it's not as if our intervention in Syria is for humanitarian reasons[27].

We summarized[28] the state of affairs in 2014:

The Syrian rebels are *mainly* Al Qaeda, and the U.S. has been supporting these terrorists[29] for years. Indeed, as reported in the Wall Street Journal[30], the National[31] and other sources, Al Qaeda's power within the Syrian rebel forces is only growing *stronger*.

Rank-and-file Syrian rebels have:

- Burned[32] American flags[33]
- Threatened to attack America[34]
- Said: "When we finish with Assad, we will fight the U.S.!" [35]
- Said: "We started our holy war here and won't finish until this [Al Qaeda] banner will be raised on top of the White House[36]. Keep funding them, you always do that, remember? Al Qaeda for instance."
- A former Syrian Jihadi says the rebels have a "9/11 ideology"[37]
- Indeed, they're *literally* singing Bin Laden's praises[38] and celebrating the 9/11 attack[39]

In fact, one of the *heads* of the Syrian rebels is also the *global boss* of Al Qaeda ... and he is calling for fresh terrorist attacks on *America*. CBS News reports[40]:

Al Qaeda chief Ayman al-Zawahiri called has called on Muslims to continue attacking Americans on their own soil in order to "bleed" the U.S. economy... "To keep up the hemorrhage in America's security and military spending, we need to keep the Unites States on a constant state of alert about where and when the next strike will blow," Zawahiri said.

Let's recap ... *Most* of the Syrian "rebels" are Al Qaeda[41]. The U.S. government has designated these guys as terrorists[42].

Things are getting worse, not better: Al Qaeda is gaining *more and more power*[43] among the rebels....

Indeed, we've long known that *most* of the weapons we're shipping to Syria are ending up in the hands of Al Qaeda[44]. And they apparently have chemical weapons[45].

Summary: We're arming the same guys who are threatening to blow us up.

Indeed, ISIS has tripled the size of its territory in Syria[46] and greatly expanded its territory in Iraq[47] even after the U.S. started its bombing campaign against ISIS. (Update: ISIS now has captured even more of Syria[48].)

Is something deeper going on behind the scene?

Part 2: ISIS' Strange Leadership

There is a question about whether the heads of ISIS are who we've been told.

For example, the New York Times reported[49] in 2007:

> For more than a year, the leader of one the most notorious insurgent groups in Iraq was said to be a mysterious Iraqi named Abdullah Rashid al-Baghdadi.
>
> As the **titular head of the Islamic State** in Iraq, an organization publicly backed by Al Qaeda, Baghdadi issued a steady stream of incendiary pronouncements. Despite claims by Iraqi officials that he had been killed in May, Baghdadi appeared to have persevered unscathed.
>
> On Wednesday, a senior American military spokesman provided a new explanation for Baghdadi's ability to escape attack: He never existed.
>
> **Brigadier General Kevin Bergner, the chief American military spokesman, said the elusive Baghdadi was actually a fictional character** whose audio-taped declarations were provided by an elderly actor named Abu Abdullah al-Naima.
>
> The ruse, Bergner said, was devised by Abu Ayub al-Masri, the Egyptian-born leader of Al Qaeda in Mesopotamia, who was trying to mask the dominant role that foreigners play in that insurgent organization.
>
> The ploy was to invent Baghdadi, a figure whose very name establishes his Iraqi pedigree, install him as the head of a front organization called the Islamic State of Iraq and then arrange for Masri to swear allegiance to him. Ayman al-Zawahiri, Osama bin

Laden's deputy, sought to reinforce the deception by referring to Baghdadi in his video and Internet statements...

Bruce Riedel, a former CIA official and a Middle East expert, said that experts had long wondered whether Baghdadi actually existed. "There has been a question mark about this," he said...

American military spokesmen insist they have gotten to the truth on Baghdadi. Mashadani, they say, provided his account because he resented the role of foreign leaders in Al Qaeda in Mesopotamia.

The unmasking of the terror leader as being an actor's fictitious persona came after al-Baghdadi was – according to mainstream media reports – arrested in 2007[50], killed in 2007[51], arrested *again*[52] in 2009, and then killed *again*[53] in 2010.

The story of ISIS' previous leader – Abu Musab al-Zarqawi – was odd as well. He was declared dead[54] in 2004. Then he was said to be arrested[55] ... several different times[56]. Then he was supposedly killed again in 2006[57].

The Independent – in an article on "black propaganda" (i.e. intentional disinformation) by the U.S. government – cites[58] the forging by the U.S. government of a letter which it pretended was written by al Zarqawi, which was then unquestioningly parroted by the media as an authentic by Zarqawi letter. The Washington Post reported[59]:

One internal briefing, produced by the U.S. military headquarters in Iraq, said that Kimmitt [Brigadier General Mark Kimmitt, the U.S. military's chief spokesman in 2004, and subsequently the senior planner on the staff of the Central Command that directs operations in Iraq and the rest of the Middle East] had concluded that, "The Zarqawi PSYOP program is the most successful information campaign to date."

And CNN reported[60] that ISIS' *current* leader – Abu Bakr al-Baghdadi – was "respected" very much by the U.S. Army and allowed to communicate freely with other prisoners in the prison in which ISIS was hatched (see Part 1) and to travel without restriction at that prison.

Part 3: Deeper Background

To understand the deeper story behind ISIS, we have to go back more than half a century to look at U.S. history in the Middle East (and drill deep down for the black gold).

Target: Iraq

Between 1932 and 1948, the roots for the current wars in Iraq were planted. As Wikipedia explains[61]:

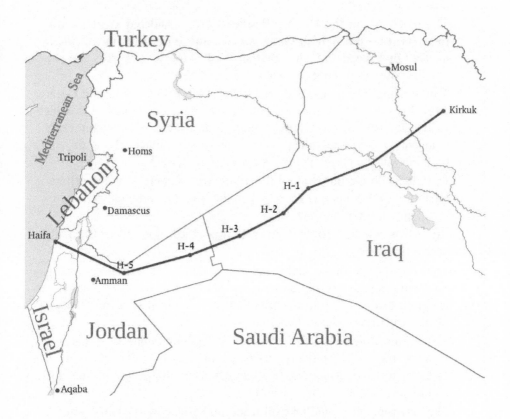

The Mosul–Haifa oil pipeline (also known as Mediterranean pipeline) was a crude oil pipeline from the oil fields in Kirkuk, located in north **Iraq**, through Jordan to Haifa (now on the territory of Israel). The pipeline was operational in 1935–1948. Its length was about 942 kilometres (585 mi), with a diameter of 12 inches (300 mm) (reducing to 10 and 8 inches (250 and 200 mm) in parts), and it took about 10 days for crude oil to travel the full length of the line. The oil arriving in Haifa was distilled in the Haifa refineries, stored in tanks, and then put in tankers for shipment to Europe.

The pipeline was built by the Iraq Petroleum Company between 1932 and 1935, during which period most of the area through which the pipeline passed was under a British mandate approved by the League of Nations. The pipeline was one of two pipelines carrying oil from the Kirkuk oilfield to the Mediterranean coast. The main pipeline split at Haditha with a second line carrying oil to Tripoli, Lebanon, which was then under a French mandate. This line was built primarily to satisfy the demands of the French partner in IPC, Compagnie Française des Pétroles, for a separate line to be built across French mandated territory.

The pipeline and the Haifa refineries were considered **strategically important by the British Government, and indeed provided much of the fuel needs of the British and American forces in the Mediterranean during the Second World War**.

The pipeline was a target of attacks by Arab gangs during the Great Arab Revolt, and as a result one of the main objectives of a joint British-Jewish Special Night Squad commanded by Captain Orde Wingate was to protect the pipeline against such attacks. Later on, the pipeline was the target of attacks by the Irgun. [Background[62].]

In 1948, with the outbreak of the 1948 Arab–Israeli War, the official operation of the pipeline ended when the Iraqi Government refused to pump any more oil through it.

Why is this relevant today? Haaretz reported[63] soon after the Iraq war started in 2003:

The United States has asked Israel to check the possibility of pumping oil from Iraq to the oil refineries in Haifa. The request came in a telegram last week from a senior Pentagon official to a top Foreign Ministry official in Jerusalem.

The Prime Minister's Office, which views the pipeline to Haifa as a "bonus" the U.S. could give to Israel in return for its unequivocal support for the American-led campaign in Iraq, had asked the Americans for the official telegram.

The new pipeline would take oil from the Kirkuk area, where some 40 percent of Iraqi oil is produced, and transport it via Mosul, and then across Jordan to Israel. **The U.S. telegram included a request for a cost estimate for repairing the Mosul-Haifa pipeline that was in use prior to 1948. During the War of Independence [what Jews call[64] the 1948 war to form the state of Israel], the Iraqis stopped the flow of oil to Haifa and the pipeline fell into disrepair over the years...**

National Infrastructure Minister Yosef Paritzky said yesterday that the port of Haifa is an attractive destination for Iraqi oil and that he plans to discuss this matter with the U.S. secretary of energy during his planned visit to Washington next month...

In response to rumors about the possible Kirkuk-Mosul-Haifa pipeline, Turkey has warned Israel that it would regard this development as a serious blow to Turkish-Israeli relations.

So the fighting over Iraq can be traced back to events occurring in 1948 and before.

But let's fast-forward to subsequent little-known events in Iraq.

The CIA plotted to poison the Iraqi leader[65] in 1960.

In 1963, the U.S. backed the coup which *succeeded*[66] in killing the head of Iraq.

And everyone knows that the U.S. also toppled Saddam Hussein during the Iraq war. But most don't know that neoconservatives planned regime change in Iraq once again in 1991[67].

4-Star General Wesley Clark – former Supreme Allied Commander of NATO – said:

It came back to me … a **1991** meeting I had with Paul Wolfowitz...

In 1991, he was the Undersecretary of Defense for Policy – the number 3 position at the Pentagon. And I had gone to see him when I was a 1-Star General commanding the National Training Center...

And I said, "Mr. Secretary, you must be pretty happy with the performance of the troops in Desert Storm." And he said: "Yeah, but not really, because the truth is we should have gotten rid of Saddam Hussein, and we didn't … But one thing we did learn [from the Persian Gulf War] is that we can use our military in the region – in the Middle East – and the Soviets won't stop us. And we've got about 5 or 10 years to clean up those old Soviet client regimes – *Syria*, Iran, *IRAQ* – before the next great superpower comes on to challenge us."

And many people don't know that the architects of the Iraq War *themselves* admitted the war was about oil[68]. For example, former U.S. Secretary of Defense – and former 12-year Republican Senator – Chuck Hagel said[69] of the Iraq war in 2007:

People say we're not fighting for oil. Of course we are. They talk about America's national interest. What the hell do you think they're talking about? We're not there for figs.

4 Star General John Abizaid – the former commander of CENTCOM with responsibility for Iraq – said[70]: "Of course it's about oil, it's very much about oil, and we can't really deny that."

Former Fed Chairman Alan Greenspan said[71] in 2007: "I am saddened that it is politically inconvenient to acknowledge what everyone knows: the Iraq war is largely about oil."

President George W. Bush said[72] in 2005 that keeping Iraqi oil away from the bad guys was a *key motive* for the Iraq war:

> If Zarqawi and [Osama] bin Laden gain control of Iraq, they would create a new training ground for future terrorist attacks. They'd seize oil fields to fund their ambitions.

John McCain said[73] in 2008:

> My friends, I will have an energy policy that we will be talking about, which will eliminate our dependence on oil from the Middle East that will — that will then prevent us — that will prevent us from having ever to send our young men and women into conflict again in the Middle East.

Sarah Palin said[74] in 2008:

> Better to start that drilling [for oil within the U.S.] today than wait and continue relying on foreign sources of energy. We are a nation at war and in many [ways] the reasons for war are fights over energy sources, which is nonsensical when you consider that domestically we have the supplies ready to go.

Former Bush speechwriter David Frum – author of the infamous "Axis of Evil" claim in Bush's 2002 State of the Union address – writes[75] in Newsweek:

> In 2002, Chalabi [the Iraqi politician and oil minister[76] who the Bush Administration favored to lead Iraq after the war] joined the annual summer retreat of the American Enterprise Institute near Vail, Colorado. He and Cheney spent long hours together, contemplating the possibilities of a Western-oriented Iraq: **an additional source of oil**, an alternative to U.S. dependency on an unstable-looking Saudi Arabia.

Key war architect – and Under Secretary of State – John Bolton said[77]:

> The critical oil and natural gas producing region that we fought so many wars to try and protect our economy from the adverse impact of losing that supply or having it available only at very high prices.

General Wesley Clark said[78] that the Iraq war – like all modern U.S. wars – were about oil.

> A high-level National Security Council officer strongly implied that Cheney and the U.S. oil chiefs planned the Iraq war before 9/11 in order to get control of its oil[79].

The Sunday Herald reported[80]:

> It is a document that fundamentally questions the motives behind the Bush administration's desire to take out Saddam Hussein and go to war with Iraq.

Strategic Energy Policy Challenges For The 21st Century
describes how America is facing the biggest energy crisis in its
history. It **targets Saddam as a threat to American interests
because of his control of Iraqi oilfields and recommends the use of
'military intervention' as a means to fix the US energy crisis**.

**The report is linked to a veritable who's who of US hawks, oilmen
and corporate bigwigs**. It was commissioned by James Baker, the
former US Secretary of State under George Bush Sr, and **submitted
to Vice-President Dick Cheney in April 2001** — a full five months
before September 11. Yet it **advocates a policy of using military
force against an enemy such as Iraq to secure US access to, and
control of, Middle Eastern oil field**s.

One of the most telling passages in the document reads: '**Iraq
remains a destabilising influence to ... the flow of oil** to
international markets from the Middle East. Saddam Hussein has also
demonstrated a willingness to threaten to use the oil weapon and to
use his own export programme to manipulate oil markets.

'This would display his personal power, enhance his image as a pan-
Arab leader ... and pressure others for a lifting of economic sanctions
against his regime. The United States should conduct an immediate
policy review toward Iraq including military, energy, economic and
political/diplomatic assessments...

'Military intervention' is supported .....

The document also points out that 'the United States remains a
prisoner of its energy dilemma', and that one of the 'consequences' of
this is a 'need for military intervention'.

**At the heart of the decision to target Iraq over oil lies dire
mismanagement of the US energy policy** over decades by
consecutive administrations. The report refers to the huge power cuts
that have affected California in recent years and warns of 'more
Californias' ahead.

It says the 'central dilemma' for the US administration is that 'the
American people continue to demand plentiful and cheap energy
without sacrifice or inconvenience'. With the 'energy sector in critical
condition, a crisis could erupt at any time [which] could have
potentially enormous impact on the US ... and would affect US
national security and foreign policy in dramatic ways.'..

The response is to put oil at the heart of the administration — 'a
reassessment of the role of energy in American foreign policy'...

Iraq is described as the world's 'key swing producer ... turning its
taps on and off when it has felt such action was in its strategic
interest". The report also says there is a 'possibility that Saddam may

remove Iraqi oil from the market for an extended period of time', creating a volatile market...

Halliburton is one of the firms thought by analysts to be in line to make a killing in any clean-up operation after another US-led war on Iraq.

All five permanent members of the UN Security Council — the UK, France, China, Russia and the US — have international oil companies that would benefit from huge windfalls in the event of regime change in Baghdad. The best chance for US firms to make billions would come if Bush installed a pro-US Iraqi opposition member as the head of a new government.

Representatives of foreign oil firms have already met with leaders of the Iraqi opposition. Ahmed Chalabi, the London-based leader of the Iraqi National Congress, said: 'American companies will have a big shot at Iraqi oil.'

The Independent reported[81] in 2011:

Plans to exploit Iraq's oil reserves were discussed by government ministers and the world's largest oil companies the year before Britain took a leading role in invading Iraq, government documents show...

The minutes of a series of meetings between ministers and senior oil executives are at odds with the public denials of self-interest from oil companies and Western governments at the time...

Minutes of a meeting with BP, Shell and BG (formerly British Gas) on 31 October 2002 read: "Baroness Symons agreed that it would be difficult to justify British companies losing out in Iraq in that way if the UK had itself been a conspicuous supporter of the US government throughout the crisis."

The minister then promised to "report back to the companies before Christmas" on her lobbying efforts.

The Foreign Office invited BP in on 6 November 2002 to talk about opportunities in Iraq "post regime change". Its minutes state: "Iraq is the big oil prospect. BP is desperate to get in there and anxious that political deals should not deny them the opportunity."

After another meeting, this one in October 2002, the Foreign Office's Middle East director at the time, Edward Chaplin, noted: "Shell and BP could not afford not to have a stake in [Iraq] for the sake of their long-term future... We were determined to get a fair slice of the action for UK companies in a post-Saddam Iraq."

Whereas BP was insisting in public that it had "no strategic interest" in Iraq, in private it told the Foreign Office that Iraq was "more important than anything we've seen for a long time".

BP was concerned that if Washington allowed TotalFinaElf's existing contact with Saddam Hussein to stand after the invasion it would make the French conglomerate the world's leading oil company. BP told the Government it was willing to take "big risks" to get a share of the Iraqi reserves, the second largest in the world.

Over 1,000 documents were obtained under Freedom of Information over five years by the oil campaigner Greg Muttitt. They reveal that at least five meetings were held between civil servants, ministers and BP and Shell in late 2002.

The 20-year contracts signed in the wake of the invasion were the largest in the history of the oil industry. They covered half of Iraq's reserves – 60 billion barrels of oil ...

[Note: The 1990 Gulf war – while not a regime change – was also about oil. Specifically, Saddam Hussein's invasion of Kuwait caused oil prices to skyrocket. The U.S. invaded Iraq in order to calm oil markets[82]. In its August 20, 1990 issue, Time Magazine quoted[83] an anonymous U.S. Official as saying:

Even a dolt understands the principle. We need the oil. It's nice to talk about standing up for freedom, but Kuwait and Saudi Arabia are not exactly democracies, and if their principal export were oranges, a mid-level State Department official would have issued a statement and we would have closed Washington down for August.]

Target: Syria

The history of western intervention in Syria is similar to our meddling in Iraq.

The CIA backed a right-wing coup in Syria in 1949[84]. Douglas Little, Professor, Department of Clark University History professor Douglas Little notes[85]:

As early as 1949, this newly independent Arab republic was an important staging ground for the CIA's earliest experiments in covert action. The CIA secretly encouraged a right-wing military coup in 1949.

The reason the U.S. initiated the coup? Little explains:

In late 1945, the Arabian American Oil Company (ARAMCO) announced plans to construct the Trans-Arabian Pipe Line (TAPLINE) from Saudi Arabia to the Mediterranean. With U.S. help, ARAMCO secured rights-of-way from Lebanon, Jordan and Saudi Arabia. The Syrian right-of-way was stalled in parliament.

In other words, Syria was the sole holdout for the lucrative oil pipeline.

The BBC reports[86] that – in 1957 – the British and American leaders seriously considered attacking the Syrian government using Muslim extremists in Syria as a form of "false flag" attack:

In 1957 Harold Macmillan [then Prime Minister of the United Kingdom] and President Dwight Eisenhower approved a CIA-MI6 plan to stage fake border incidents as an excuse for an invasion by Syria's pro-western neighbours, and then to "eliminate" the most influential triumvirate in Damascus.... More importantly, Syria also had control of one of the main oil arteries of the Middle East, the pipeline which connected pro-western Iraq's oilfields to Turkey...

The report said that once the necessary degree of fear had been created, frontier incidents and border clashes would be staged to provide a pretext for Iraqi and Jordanian military intervention. Syria had to be "made to appear as the sponsor of plots, sabotage and violence directed against neighbouring governments," the report says. "CIA and SIS should use their capabilities in both the psychological and action fields to augment tension." That meant operations in Jordan, Iraq, and Lebanon, taking the form of "sabotage, national conspiracies and various strong-arm activities" to be blamed on Damascus. The plan called for funding of a **"Free Syria Committee"** [hmmm ... sounds vaguely familiar[87]], and the **arming of "political factions with paramilitary or other actionist capabilities" within Syria**. The CIA and MI6 would **instigate internal uprisings**, for instance by **the Druze** [a Shia Muslim sect[88]] in the south, help to free political prisoners held in the Mezze prison, **and stir up the Muslim Brotherhood in Damascus**.

Neoconservatives planned regime change in Syria once again in 1991[89] (as noted above in the quote from 4-Star General Wesley Clark).

And as the Guardian reported[90] in 2013:

According to former French foreign minister Roland Dumas[91], Britain had planned covert action in Syria as early as 2009:

"I was in England two years before the violence in Syria on other business," he told French television: "I met with top British officials, who confessed to me that they were preparing something in Syria. This was in Britain not in America. Britain was preparing gunmen to invade Syria.."

Leaked emails from the private intelligence firm Stratfor[92], including notes from a meeting with Pentagon officials[93], confirmed that as of 2011, US and UK special forces training of Syrian opposition forces was well underway. The goal was to elicit the "collapse" of Assad's regime "from within.."

In 2009 – the same year former French foreign minister Dumas alleges the British began planning operations in Syria – Assad refused to sign[94] a proposed agreement with Qatar that would run a pipeline from the latter's North field[95], contiguous with Iran's South Pars field, through Saudi Arabia, Jordan, Syria and on to Turkey, with a view to supply European markets – albeit crucially bypassing Russia. Assad's rationale was "to protect the interests of [his] Russian ally, which is Europe's top supplier of natural gas."

Instead, the following year, Assad pursued negotiations for an alternative $10 billion pipeline plan with Iran[96], across Iraq to Syria, that would also potentially allow Iran to supply gas to Europe from its South Pars field shared with Qatar. The Memorandum of Understanding (MoU) for the project was signed in July 2012 – just as Syria's civil war was spreading to Damascus and Aleppo – and earlier this year Iraq signed a framework agreement for construction of the gas pipelines[97].

The Iran-Iraq-Syria pipeline plan was a "direct slap in the face[98]" to Qatar's plans. No wonder Saudi Prince Bandar bin Sultan, in a failed attempt to bribe Russia to switch sides, told President Vladimir Putin that "whatever regime comes after" Assad, it will be "completely" in Saudi Arabia's hands[99] and will "not sign any agreement allowing any Gulf country to transport its gas across Syria to Europe and compete with Russian gas exports", according to diplomatic sources. When Putin refused, the Prince vowed military action.

It would seem that contradictory self-serving Saudi and Qatari oil interests are pulling the strings of an equally self-serving oil-focused US policy in Syria, if not the wider region. It is this – the problem of establishing a pliable opposition which the US and its oil allies feel confident will play ball[100], pipeline-style, in a post-Assad Syria – that will determine the nature of any prospective intervention: not concern for Syrian life.

[Footnote: The U.S. and its allies have toppled many other governments, as well[101].]

The war in Syria – like Iraq – is largely about oil and gas.
International Business Times noted[102] in 2013:

[Syria] controls one of the largest conventional hydrocarbon resources in the eastern Mediterranean.

Syria possessed 2.5 billion barrels of crude oil as of January 2013, which makes it the largest proved reserve of crude oil in the eastern Mediterranean according to the Oil & Gas Journal estimate...

Syria also has oil shale resources with estimated reserves that range as high as 50 billion tons, according to a Syrian government source in 2010.

Moreover, Syria is a key chess piece[103] in the pipeline wars. Syria is an integral part[104] of the proposed 1,200km Arab Gas Pipeline:

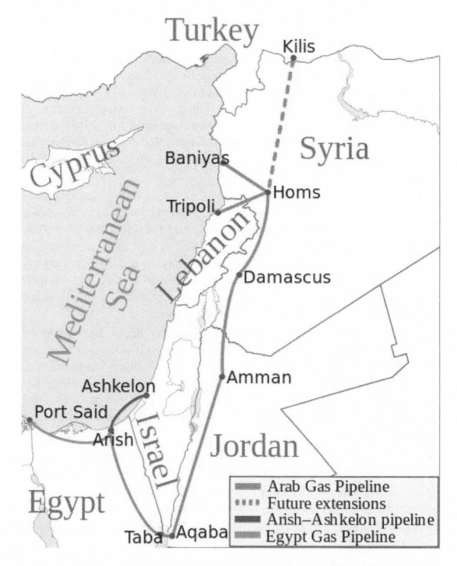

Here are some additional graphics[105] courtesy of Adam Curry:

http://blog.curry.com/images/2012/02/07/arabGasPipeline.jpg

http://blog.curry.com/images/2012/02/07/syria-turkey.jpg and

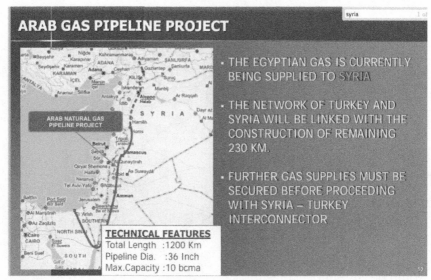

http://blog.curry.com/images/2012/02/07/levantprovince2.jpg,

Syria's central role in the Arab gas pipeline is also a key to why it is now being targeted.

Just as the Taliban was scheduled for removal after they demanded too much in return for the Unocal pipeline, Syria's Assad is being targeted because he is not a reliable "player".

Specifically, **Turkey, Israel and their ally the U.S. want an assured flow of gas through Syria**, and don't want a Syrian regime which is not unquestionably loyal to those 3 countries to stand in the way of the pipeline ... or which demands too big a cut of the profits.

A deal has also been inked to run a natural gas pipeline from Iran's giant South Pars field through Iraq and Syria[106] (with a possible extension to Lebanon). And a deal to run petroleum from Iraq's Kirkuk oil field to the Syrian port of Banias has also been approved:

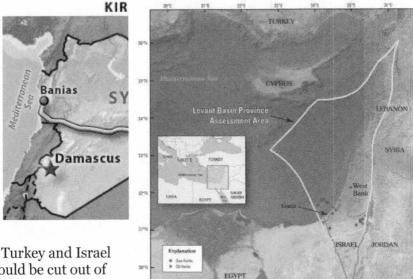

Turkey and Israel
would be cut out of
these competing
pipelines.

Gail Tverberg- an
expert on financial aspects of the oil industry – writes[107]:

> One of the limits in ramping up Iraqi oil extraction is the limited
> amount of infrastructure available for exporting oil from Iraq. If
> pipelines through **Syria** could be added, this might alleviate part of
> the problem in getting oil to international markets.

The Plan to Break Up Iraq and Syria?

In September 2015, Pentagon intelligence chief Lt. Gen. Vincent
Stewart said[108] that he has "a tough time" seeing either Iraq or Syria
really coming back together as sovereign nations. This may sound like
a reaction to ISIS and the civil war raging in Syria. But – in reality –
the hawks in the U.S. and Israel decided long ago[109] to break up Iraq
and Syria into small fragments.

The Guardian noted[110] in 2003:

> President Hosni Mubarak of Egypt predicted devastating
> consequences for the Middle East if Iraq is attacked. "We fear a state
> of disorder and chaos may prevail in the region," he said...

> They are probably still splitting their sides with laughter in the
> Pentagon. But Mr Mubarak and the [Pentagon] hawks do agree on one
> thing: war with Iraq could spell disaster for several regimes in the
> Middle East. Mr Mubarak believes that would be bad. **The hawks,
> though, believe it would be good**.

For the hawks, disorder and chaos sweeping through the region would not be an unfortunate side-effect of war with Iraq, but a sign that **everything is going according to plan**...

The "skittles theory" of the Middle East – that one ball aimed at Iraq can knock down several regimes – has been around for some time on the wilder fringes of politics but has come to the fore in the United States on the back of the "war against terrorism".

Its roots can be traced, at least in part, to a paper published in 1996 by an Israeli think tank, the Institute for Advanced Strategic and Political Studies. Entitled "A clean break: a new strategy for securing the realm", it was intended as a political **blueprint for the incoming government of Binyamin Netanyahu**. As the title indicates, it advised the right-wing Mr Netanyahu to make a complete break with the past by adopting a strategy "based on an entirely new intellectual foundation, one that restores strategic initiative and provides the nation the room to engage every possible energy on rebuilding Zionism …"..

The paper set out a plan by which Israel would "shape its strategic environment", beginning with the removal of Saddam Hussein and the installation of a Hashemite monarchy in Baghdad.

With Saddam out of the way and Iraq thus brought under Jordanian Hashemite influence, Jordan and Turkey would form an axis along with Israel to weaken and "roll back" Syria. Jordan, it suggested, could also sort out Lebanon by "weaning" the Shia Muslim population away from Syria and Iran, and re-establishing their former ties with the Shia in the new Hashemite kingdom of Iraq. "Israel will not only contain its foes; it will transcend them", the paper concluded...

The leader of the "prominent opinion makers" who wrote it was **Richard Perle – now chairman of the Defense Policy Board at the Pentagon**.

Also among the eight-person team was **Douglas Feith, a neo-conservative lawyer, who now holds one of the top four posts at the Pentagon as under-secretary of policy**...

Two other opinion-makers in the team were **David Wurmser and his wife, Meyrav** (see US thinktanks give lessons in foreign policy[111], August 19). Mrs Wurmser was co-founder of Memri, a Washington-based charity that distributes articles translated from Arabic newspapers portraying Arabs in a bad light. After working with Mr Perle at the American Enterprise Institute, David Wurmser is now at the State Department, as a special assistant to John Bolton, the under-secretary for arms control and international security.

A fifth member of the team was James Colbert, of the Washington-based Jewish Institute for National Security Affairs (Jinsa) – a bastion of neo-conservative hawkery whose advisory board was previously graced by Dick Cheney (now US vice-president), John Bolton and Douglas Feith...

With several of the "Clean Break" paper's authors now holding key positions in Washington, the plan for Israel to "transcend" its foes by reshaping the Middle East looks a good deal more achievable today than it did in 1996. Americans may even be persuaded to give up their lives to achieve it.

(Before assuming prominent roles in the Bush administration, many of the same people – including Richard Perle, Paul Wolfowitz, Dick Cheney, John Bolton and others[112] – advocated their imperial views during the Clinton administration via their American think tank, the "Project for a New American Century".)

Thomas Harrington – professor of Iberian Studies at Trinity College in Hartford, Connecticut – writes[113]:

[While there are some good articles on the chaos in Iraq, none of them] consider whether **the chaos now enveloping the region might, in fact, be the desired aim of policy planners in Washington and Tel Aviv...**

One of the prime goals of every empire is to foment ongoing internecine conflict in the territories whose resources and/or strategic outposts they covet...

The most efficient way of sparking such open-ended internecine conflict is to brutally smash the target country's social matrix and physical infrastructure...

Ongoing unrest has the additional perk of justifying the maintenance and expansion of the military machine that feeds the financial and political fortunes of the metropolitan elite.

In short ... divide and rule is about as close as it gets to a universal recourse the imperial game and that it is, therefore, as important to bear it in mind today as it was in the times of Alexander the Great, Julius Caesar, the Spanish Conquistadors and the British Raj.

To those—and I suspect there are still many out there—for whom all this seems too neat or too *conspiratorial*, I would suggest a careful side-by side reading of:

a) the "Clean Break" manifesto generated by the Jerusalem-based Institute for Advanced Strategic and Political Studies (IASPS) in 1996 and

b) the "Rebuilding America's Defenses" paper generated by The Project for a New American Century (PNAC) in 2000, a US group with deep personal and institutional links to the aforementioned Israeli think tank, and with the ascension of George Bush Junior to the White House, to the most exclusive sanctums of the US foreign policy apparatus.

To read the cold-blooded imperial reasoning in both of these documents—which speak, in the first case, quite openly of **the need to destabilize the region** so as to reshape Israel's "strategic environment" and, in the second of the need to dramatically increase the number of US "forward bases" in the region ….

To do so now, after the US's systematic destruction of Iraq and Libya—two notably oil-rich countries whose delicate ethnic and religious balances were well known to anyone in or out of government with more than passing interest in history—, and after them its carefully calibrated efforts to generate and maintain murderous and civilization-destroying stalemates in Syria and Egypt (something that is easily substantiated despite our media's deafening silence on the subject), is downright blood-curdling.

And yet, it seems that for even very well-informed analysts, it is beyond the pale to raise the possibility that foreign policy elites in the US and Israel, like all virtually all the ambitious hegemons before them on the world stage, might have quite coldly and consciously fomented open-ended chaos in order to achieve their overlapping strategic objectives in this part of the world.

Antiwar's Justin Raimondo notes[114]:

Iraq's fate was sealed from the moment we invaded: it has no future as a unitary state. As I pointed out again[115] and again[116] in the early days of the conflict, Iraq is fated to split apart into at least three separate states: the Shi'ite areas around Baghdad and to the south, the Sunni regions to the northwest, and the Kurdish enclave which was itching for independence since well before the US invasion. **This was the War Party's real[117] if unexpressed goal from the very beginning: the atomization of Iraq, and indeed the entire Middle East. Their goal, in short, was chaos** – and that is precisely what we are seeing today...

As I put it years ago[118]:

"[T]he actual purpose was to blow the country to smithereens: to atomize it, and crush it, so that it would never rise again.

"When we invaded and occupied Iraq, we didn't just militarily defeat Iraq's armed forces – we dismantled their army[119], and their police force, along with all the other institutions that held the country

together. The educational system was destroyed, and not reconstituted. The infrastructure was pulverized[120], and never restored. Even the physical hallmarks of a civilized society – roads[121], bridges[122], electrical plants[123], water facilities[124], museums[125], schools[126] – were bombed out of existence or else left to fall into disrepair. Along with that, the spiritual and psychological infrastructure that enables a society to function – the bonds of trust, allegiance, and custom – was dissolved[127], leaving Iraqis to fend for themselves in a war of all against all.

"… What we are witnessing in post-Saddam Iraq is the erasure of an entire country. We can say, with confidence: We came, we saw, we atomized."

Why? This is the question that inevitably arises in the wake of such an analysis: why deliberately destroy an entire country whose people were civilized while our European ancestors were living in trees?

The people who planned, agitated for, and executed this war are the very same people who have advanced Israeli interests – at America's expense – at every opportunity. In "A Clean Break: A New Strategy for Securing the Realm[128]," a 1996 document prepared by a gaggle of neocons – Perle, Douglas Feith, James Colbert, Charles Fairbanks, Jr., Robert Loewenberg, David Wurmser, and Meyrav Wurmser – Israeli Prime Minister Benjamin Netanyahu was urged to "break out" -of Israel's alleged stagnation and undertake a campaign of "regime change" across the Middle East, targeting Lebanon, Libya, Syria, Iraq, and eventually Iran. With the exception of Iran – and that one's still cooking on the back burner – this is precisely what has occurred. In 2003, in the immediate wake of our Pyrrhic "victory" in Iraq, then Prime Minister Ariel Sharon declared[129] to a visiting delegation of American members of Congress that these "rogue states" – Iran, Libya, and Syria – would have to be next on the War Party's target list.

(Indeed[130].)

And Michel Chossudovsky points out[131]:

The division of Iraq along sectarian-ethnic lines has been on the drawing board of the Pentagon for more than 10 years.

What is envisaged by Washington is the outright suppression of the Baghdad regime and the institutions of the central government, leading to a process of political fracturing and **the elimination of Iraq as a country**.

This process of political fracturing in Iraq along sectarian lines will inevitably have an impact on Syria, where the US-NATO sponsored terrorists have in large part been defeated.

Destabilization and political fragmentation in Syria is also contemplated: Washington's intent is no longer to pursue the narrow objective of "regime change" in Damascus. What is contemplated is the break up of both Iraq and Syria along sectarian-ethnic lines.

The formation of the caliphate may be the first step towards a broader conflict in the Middle East, bearing in mind that Iran is supportive of the al-Maliki government and the US ploy may indeed be to encourage the intervention of Iran.

The proposed re-division of both Iraq and Syria is broadly modeled on that of the Federation of Yugoslavia (leader of the non-aligned bloc) which was split up by internecine warfare into seven "independent states" (Serbia, Croatia, Bosnia-Herzegovina, Macedonia (FYRM), Slovenia, Montenegro, Kosovo). According to Mahdi Darius Nazemroaya, the division of Iraq into three separate states is part of a broader process of redrawing the Map of the Middle East.

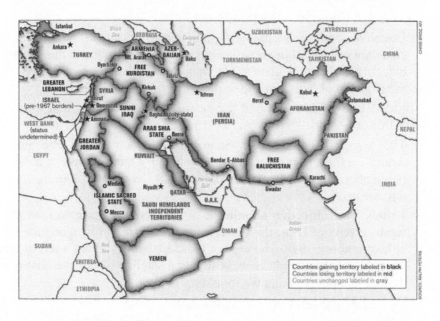

The above map was prepared by Lieutenant Colonel Ralph Peters. It was published in the Armed Forces Journal in June 2006, Peters is a retired colonel of the U.S. National War Academy. (Map Copyright Lt. Colonel Ralph Peters 2006).

Although the map does not officially reflect Pentagon doctrine, it has been used in a training program at NATO's Defense College for senior military officers". (See Plans for Redrawing the Middle East:

The Project for a "New Middle East"[132] *By Mahdi Darius Nazemroaya[133], Global Research, November 2006)*

Similarly, Neooconservatives in the U.S. and Israel have long advocated for the balkanization of Syria into smaller regions based on ethnicity and religion. The goal was to *break up* the country, and to do away with the sovereignty of Syria as a separate nation.

In 1982, a prominent Israeli journalist formerly attached to the Israeli Foreign Ministry wrote[134] a book expressly calling for the break-up of Syria:

> All the Arab states should be broken down, by Israel, into small units .... **Dissolution of Syria** and Iraq later on **into ethnically or religiously unique areas such** as in Lebanon, is Israel's primary target on the Eastern front in the long run.

In any event, it is well-documented that – in 1996 – U.S. and Israeli Neocons advocated[135] "Weakening, containing, and even **rolling back** Syria..."

As Michel Chossudovsky points out[136]:

> Destabilization and political fragmentation in Syria is also contemplated: Washington's intent is no longer to pursue the narrow objective of "regime change" in Damascus. What is contemplated is the break up of both Iraq and Syria along sectarian-ethnic lines.

Indeed, in May 2015, one of the key architects[137] of the Iraq war – John Bolton – said:[138]

> The Arabs divided between Sunnis and Shias – I think the Sunni Arabs are never going to agree to be in a state where the Shia outnumber them 3-1. That's what ISIS has been able to take advantage of.
>
> I think **our objective should be a new Sunni state out of the western part of Iraq, the eastern part of Syria** run by moderates or at least authoritarians who are not radical Islamists. What's left of the state of Iraq, as of right now, is simply a satellite of the ayatollahs in Tehran. It's not anything we should try to aid.

U.S. and Allied Support for Extremists

There's one more historical fact which is key background to understanding ISIS: U.S. and allied support for extremists.

Front row, from left: Major Gen. Hamid Gul, director general of Pakistan's Inter-Services Intelligence Directorate (ISI), **Director of Central Intelligence Agency (CIA) William Webster**; **Deputy Director for Operations Clair George**; an ISI colonel; and senior CIA official, Milt Bearden at a Mujahideen training camp in North-West Frontier Province of Pakistan in 1987. (source RAWA)

Ronald Reagan meets Afghan Mujahideen Commanders at the White House in 1985 (Reagan Archives[139])

We Created Al Qaeda to Fight the Soviets in Afghanistan

Jimmy Carter's National Security Adviser Zbigniew Brzezinski admitted[140] on CNN that the U.S. organized and supported Bin Laden and the other originators of "Al Qaeda" in the 1970s[141] to fight the Soviets.

Brzezinski told[142] Al Qaeda's forefathers – the Mujahedin:

> We know of their deep belief in god – that they're confident that their struggle will succeed. That land over – there is yours – and you'll go back to it some day, because your fight will prevail, and you'll have your homes, your mosques, back again, because your cause is right, and god is on your side.

CIA director and Secretary of Defense Robert Gates confirmed[143] in his memoir that the U.S. backed the Mujahedin in the 1970s.

Former Secretary of State Hillary Clinton agrees[144].

MSNBC reported[145] in 1998:

> As his unclassified CIA biography states, bin Laden left Saudi Arabia to fight the Soviet army in Afghanistan after Moscow's invasion in 1979. By 1984, he was running a front organization known as Maktab al-Khidamar – the MAK – which funneled money, arms and fighters from the outside world into the Afghan war.
>
> What the CIA bio conveniently fails to specify (in its unclassified form, at least) is that the MAK was nurtured by Pakistan's state security services, the Inter-Services Intelligence agency, or ISI, the CIA's primary conduit for conducting the covert war against Moscow's occupation...
>
> The CIA, concerned about the factionalism of Afghanistan ... found that Arab zealots who flocked to aid the Afghans were easier to "read" than the rivalry-ridden natives. While the Arab volunteers might well prove troublesome later, the agency reasoned, they at least were one-dimensionally anti-Soviet for now. So bin Laden, along with a small group of Islamic militants from Egypt, Pakistan, Lebanon, Syria and Palestinian refugee camps all over the Middle East, became the "reliable" partners of the CIA in its war against Moscow...
>
> To this day, those involved in the decision to give the Afghan rebels access to a fortune in covert funding and top-level combat weaponry continue to defend that move in the context of the Cold War. Sen. Orrin Hatch, a senior Republican on the Senate Intelligence Committee making those decisions, told my colleague Robert

Windrem that he would make the same call again today even knowing what bin Laden would do subsequently. "It was worth it," he said.

"Those were very important, pivotal matters that played an important role in the downfall of the Soviet Union," he said.

Indeed, the U.S. started backing Al Qaeda's forefathers *even before the Soviets invaded* Afghanistan. As Brzezinski told[146] *Le Nouvel Observateur* in a 1998 interview:

> Question: The former director of the CIA, Robert Gates, stated in his memoirs ["From the Shadows"], that **American intelligence services began to aid the Mujahadeen in Afghanistan 6 months before the Soviet intervention**. In this period you were the national security adviser to President Carter. You therefore played a role in this affair. Is that correct?

> Brzezinski: Yes. According to the official version of history, CIA aid to the Mujahadeen began during 1980, that is to say, after the Soviet army invaded Afghanistan, 24 Dec 1979. But **the reality, secretly guarded until now, is completely otherwise Indeed, it was July 3, 1979 that President Carter signed the first directive for secret aid to the opponents of the pro-Soviet regime in Kabul. And that very day, I wrote a note to the president in which I explained to him that in my opinion this aid was going to induce a Soviet military intervention...**

> Q: And neither do you regret having supported the Islamic fundamentalism, having given arms and advice to future terrorists?

> B: What is most important to the history of the world? The Taliban or the collapse of the Soviet empire? Some stirred-up Moslems or the liberation of Central Europe and the end of the Cold War?

The Washington Post reported[147] in 2002:

> The United States spent millions of dollars to supply Afghan schoolchildren with textbooks filled with violent images and militant Islamic teachings ....

> The primers, which were filled with talk of jihad and featured drawings of guns, bullets, soldiers and mines, have served since then as the Afghan school system's core curriculum. Even the Taliban used the American-produced books ....

The Council on Foreign Relations notes[148]:

> The 9/11 Commission report (PDF)[149] released in 2004 said some of Pakistan's religious schools or madrassas served as "incubators for violent extremism." Since then, there has been much debate over madrassas and their connection to militancy...

New madrassas sprouted, funded and supported by Saudi Arabia and U.S. Central Intelligence Agency, where students were encouraged to join the Afghan resistance.

And see this[150]. Veteran journalist Robert Dreyfuss[151] writes:

For half a century the United States and many of its allies saw what I call the "Islamic right" as convenient partners in the Cold War...

In the decades before 9/11, hard-core activists and organizations among Muslim fundamentalists on the far right were often viewed as allies for two reasons, because they were seen a fierce anti-communists and because the opposed secular nationalists such as Egypt's Gamal Abdel Nasser, Iran's Mohammed Mossadegh...

By the end of the 1950s, rather than allying itself with the secular forces of progress in the Middle East and the Arab world, the United States found itself in league with Saudi Arabia's Islamist legions. Choosing Saudi Arabia over Nasser's Egypt was probably the single biggest mistake the United States has ever made in the Middle East.

A second big mistake ... occurred in the 1970s, when, at the height of the Cold War and the struggle for control of the Middle East, the United States either supported or acquiesced in the rapid growth of Islamic right in countries from Egypt to Afghanistan. In Egypt, Anwar Sadat brought the Muslim Brotherhood back to Egypt. In Syria, the United States, Israel, and Jordan supported the Muslim Brotherhood in a civil war against Syria. And ... Israel quietly backed Ahmed Yassin and the Muslim Brotherhood in the West Bank and Gaza, leading to the establishment of Hamas.

Still another major mistake was the fantasy that Islam would penetrate the USSR and unravel the Soviet Union in Asia. It led to America's support for the jihadists in Afghanistan. But ... America's alliance with the Afghan Islamists long predated the Soviet invasion of Afghanistan in 1979 and had its roots in CIA activity in Afghanistan in the 1960s and in the early and mid-1970s. The Afghan jihad spawned civil war in Afghanistan in the late 1980s, gave rise to the Taliban, and got Osama bin Laden started on building Al Qaeda.

Would the Islamic right have existed without U.S. support? Of course. This is not a book for the conspiracy-minded. But there is no question that the virulence of the movement that we now confront—and which confronts many of the countries in the region, too, from Algeria to India and beyond—would have been significantly less had the United States made other choices during the Cold War.

In other words, if the U.S. and our allies hadn't backed the radical violent Muslims instead of more stable, peaceful groups in the Middle East, radical Islam wouldn't have grown so large.

Pakistani nuclear scientist and peace activist[152] Pervez Hoodbhoy writes[153]:

> Every religion, including Islam, has its crazed fanatics. Few in numbers and small in strength, they can properly be assigned to the "loony" section. This was true for Islam as well until 1979, the year of the Soviet invasion of Afghanistan. Indeed, there may well have been no 911 but for this game-changer...

> Officials like Richard Perle, Assistant Secretary of Defense, immediately saw Afghanistan not as the locale of a harsh and dangerous conflict to be ended but as a place to teach the Russians a lesson. Such "bleeders" became the most influential people in Washington...

> The task of creating such solidarity fell upon Saudi Arabia, together with other conservative Arab monarchies. This duty was accepted readily and they quickly made the Afghan Jihad their central cause.... But still more importantly, to go heart and soul for jihad was crucial at a time when Saudi legitimacy as the guardians of Islam was under strong challenge by Iran, which pointed to the continued occupation of Palestine by America's partner, Israel. An increasing number of Saudis were becoming disaffected by the House of Saud – its corruption, self-indulgence, repression, and closeness to the US. Therefore, the Jihad in Afghanistan provided an excellent outlet for the growing number of militant Sunni activists in Saudi Arabia, and a way to deal with the daily taunts of the Iranian clergy...

> The bleeders soon organized and armed the Great Global Jihad, funded by Saudi Arabia, and executed by Pakistan. **A powerful magnet for militant Sunni activists was created by the US. The most hardened and ideologically dedicated men were sought on the logic that they would be the best fighters. Advertisements, paid for from CIA funds, were placed in newspapers and newsletters around the world offering inducements and motivations to join the Jihad.**

> **American universities produced books for Afghan children that extolled the virtues of jihad and of killing communists. Readers browsing through book bazaars in Rawalpindi and Peshawar can, even today, sometimes find textbooks produced as part of the series underwritten by a USAID $50 million grant to the University of Nebraska in the 1980's . These textbooks sought to counterbalance Marxism through creating enthusiasm in Islamic militancy. They exhorted Afghan children to "pluck out the eyes of the Soviet enemy and cut off his legs". Years after the books were first printed they were approved by the Taliban for use in**

madrassas – a stamp of their ideological correctness and they are still widely available in both Afghanistan and Pakistan.

At the international level, Radical Islam went into overdrive as its superpower ally, the United States, funneled support to the mujahideen. Ronald Reagan feted jihadist leaders on the White House lawn, and the U.S. press lionized them.

And the chief of the visa section at the U.S. consulate in Jeddah, Saudi Arabia (J. Michael Springmann, who is now an attorney in private practice) says[154] that the CIA insisted that visas be issued to Afghanis so they could travel to the U.S. to be trained in terrorism in the United States, and then sent back to Afghanistan to fight the Soviets.

1993 World Trade Center Bombing

New York District Attorney Robert M. Morgenthau believed that the intelligence services could and should have stopped the 1993 bombing of the World Trade Center, but they were preoccupied with other issues cover.

As well-known[155] investigative journalist Robert I. Friedman wrote[156] in New York Magazine in 1995:

Sheikh Omar Abdel Rahman commands an almost deified adoration and respect in certain Islamic circles. It was his 1980 fatwa – religious decree – condemning Anwar Sadat for making peace with Israel that is widely believed to be responsible for Sadat's assassination a year later. (Rahman was subsequently tried but acquitted.)..

The CIA paid to send Abdel Rahman to Peshawar 'to preach to the Afghans about the necessity of unity to overthrow the Kabul regime,' according to Professor Rubin. By all accounts, Rahman was brilliant at inspiring the faithful.

As a reward for his services, the CIA gave the sheikh a one-year visa to the United States in May, 1990 – even though he was on a State Department terrorism watch list that should have barred him from the country.

After a public outcry in the wake of the World Trade Centre bombing, a State Department representative discovered that Rahman had, in fact, received four United States visas dating back to December 15, 1986. All were given to him by CIA agents acting as consular officers at American embassies in Khartoum and Cairo. The CIA officers claimed they didn't know the sheikh was one of the most notorious political figures in the Middle East and a militant on the State Department's list of undesirables. The agent in Khartoum said that when the sheikh walked in the computers were down and the Sudanese clerk didn't bother to check the microfiche file.

Says one top New York investigator: 'Left with the choice between pleading stupidity or else admitting deceit, the CIA went with stupidity.'..

The sheikh arrived in Brooklyn at a fortuitous time for the CIA. In the wake of the Soviet Union's retreat from Afghanistan, Congress had slashed the amount of covert aid going to the mujaheddin. The international network of Arab-financed support groups became even more vital to the CIA, including the string of jihad offices that had been set up across America with the help of Saudi and American intelligence. To drum up support, the agency paved the way for veterans of the Afghan conflict to visit the centres and tell their inspirational war stories; in return, the centres collected millions of dollars for the rebels at a time when they needed it most.

There were jihad offices in Jersey City, Atlanta and Dallas, but the most important was the one in Brooklyn, called Alkifah – Arabic for 'the struggle.' That storefront became the de facto headquarters of the sheikh...

On November 5, 1990, Rabbi Meir Kahane, an ultra-right-wing Zionist militant, was shot in the throat with a .357 magnum in a Manhattan hotel; El-Sayyid Nosair was gunned down by an off-duty postal inspector outside the hotel, and the murder weapon was found a few feet from his hand.

A subsequent search of Nosair's Cliffside Park, New Jersey home turned up forty boxes of evidence – evidence that, had the D.A.'s office and the FBI looked at it more carefully, would have revealed an active terrorist conspiracy about to boil over in New York...

In addition to discovering thousands of rounds of ammunition and hit lists with the names of New York judges and prosecutors, investigators found amongst the Nosair evidence classified U.S. military-training manuals...

Also found amongst Nosair's effects were several documents, letters and notebooks in Arabic, which when eventually translated would point to e terror conspiracy against the United States. The D.A.'s office shipped these, along with the other evidence, to the FBI's office at 26 Federal Plaza. 'We gave all this stuff to the bureau, thinking that they were well equipped,' says one source close to the D.A.'s office. 'After the World Trade Centre, we discovered they never translated the material.'

According to other sources familiar with the case, **the FBI told District Attorney Robert M. Morgenthau that Nosair was a lone**

**gunman, not part of a broader conspiracy; the prosecution took
this position at trial and lost, only convicting Nosair of gun
charges. Morgenthau speculated the CIA may have encouraged
the FBI not to pursue any other leads, these sources say. 'The FBI
lied to me,' Morgenthau has told colleagues. 'They're supposed to
untangle terrorist connections, but they can't be trusted to do the
job.'**

Three years later, on the day the FBI arrested four Arabs for the
World Trade Centre bombing, saying it had all of the suspects,
Morgenthau's ears pricked up. He didn't believe the four were 'self-
starters,' and speculated that there was probably a larger network as
well as a foreign sponsor. He also had a hunch that the suspects would
lead back to Sheikh Abdel Rahman. But he worried that **the dots
might not be connected because the U.S. government was
protecting the sheikh for his help in Afghanistan...**

Nevertheless, **some in the D.A.'s office believe that until the Ryder
van exploded underneath New York's tallest building, the sheikh
and his men were being protected by the CIA. Morgenthau
reportedly believes the CIA brought the sheikh to Brooklyn in the
first place....**

As far as can be determined, no American agency is investigating
leads suggesting foreign-government involvement in the New York
terror conspiracy. For example, **Saudi intelligence has contributed
to Sheikh Rahman's legal defense fund, according to Mohammed
al-Khilewi**, the former first secretary to the Saudi mission at the U.N.

Friedman notes that intelligence agents had possession of notes
which should have linked all of these terrorists, but failed to connect
the dots prior to 1993.

CNN ran a special report in 1994 called "Terror Nation? U.S.
Creation?"[157], which noted – as summarized by Congressman Peter
Deutsch[158]:

> Some Afghan groups that have had close affiliation with Pakistani
> Intelligence are believed to have been involved in the [1993] New
> York World Trade Center bombings...
>
> Pro-Western afghan officials ... officially warned the U.S.
> government about Hekmatyar no fewer than four times. The last
> warning delivered just days before the [1993] Trade Center attack."
> Speaking to former CIA Director Robert Gates, about Gulbuddin
> Hekmatyar, Peter Arnett reports, "The Pakistanis showered Gulbuddin
> Hekmatyar with U.S. provided weapons and sang his praises to the
> CIA. They had close ties with Hekmatyar going back to the mid-
> 1970's."

This is interesting because it is widely acknowledged that *Gulbuddin Hekmatyar* was enthusiastically backed by the U.S. For example, U.S. News and World Report says[159]:

> [He was] once among America's most valued allies. In the 1980s, the CIA funneled hundreds of millions of dollars in weapons and ammunition to help them battle the Soviet Army during its occupation of Afghanistan. Hekmatyar, then widely considered by Washington to be a reliable anti-Soviet rebel, was even flown to the United States by the CIA in 1985.

As the New York Times[160], CBS News[161] and others reported, an FBI informant involved in the 1993 bombing of the World Trade Center begged the FBI to substitute fake bomb power for real explosives, but his FBI handler somehow let real explosives be used.

Bosnia

As professor of strategy at the Naval War College and former National Security Agency intelligence analyst and counterintelligence officer John R. Schindler documents, the U.S. supported Bin Laden and other Al Qaeda terrorists in Bosnia[162].

Libya

We reported[163] in 2012 that the U.S. supported Al Qaeda in Libya in its effort to topple Gaddafi:

> The U.S.-supported opposition which overthrew Libya's Gaddafi was largely comprised of Al Qaeda terrorists[164]. According to a 2007 report[165] by West Point's Combating Terrorism Center's center, the Libyan city of Benghazi was one of Al Qaeda's main headquarters – and bases for sending Al Qaeda fighters into Iraq – prior to the overthrow of Gaddafi:

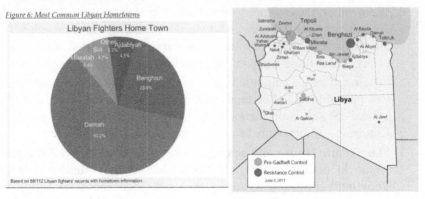

Figure 6: Most Common Libyan Hometowns

The Hindustan Times reported[166] last year:

"There is no question that al Qaeda's Libyan franchise, Libyan Islamic Fighting Group, is a part of the opposition," Bruce Riedel, former CIA officer and a leading expert on terrorism, told Hindustan Times... It has always been Qaddafi's biggest enemy and its stronghold is Benghazi.

Al Qaeda is now largely in control of Libya. Indeed, Al Qaeda flags were flown over the Benghazi courthouse[167] once Gaddafi was toppled.

(Incidentally, Gaddafi was on the verge of invading Benghazi in 2011, 4 years after the West Point report cited Benghazi as a hotbed of Al Qaeda terrorists. Gaddafi claimed – rightly it turns out – that Benghazi was an Al Qaeda stronghold and a main source of the Libyan rebellion. But NATO planes stopped him[168], and protected Benghazi.)

Former top military and CIA officers said that the U.S intentionally armed Al Qaeda in Libya. The Daily Mail reported[169] in 2014:

A self-selected group of former top military officers, CIA insiders and think-tankers, declared Tuesday in Washington that a seven-month review of the deadly 2012 terrorist attack has determined that it could have been prevented – if the **U.S.** hadn't been **helping to arm al-Qaeda militias throughout Libya** a year earlier.

'The United States switched sides in the war on terror with what we did in Libya, knowingly facilitating the provision of weapons to known al-Qaeda militias and figures,' Clare Lopez, a member of the commission and a **former CIA officer**, told MailOnline.

She blamed the Obama administration for failing to stop half of a $1 billion United Arab Emirates arms shipment from reaching al-Qaeda-linked militants.

'Remember, these weapons that came into Benghazi were permitted to enter by our armed forces who were blockading the approaches from air and sea,' Lopez claimed. 'They were permitted to come in. ... [They] knew these weapons were coming in, and that was allowed..

'The intelligence community was part of that, the Department of State was part of that, and certainly that means that the top leadership of the United States, our national security leadership, and potentially Congress – if they were briefed on this – also knew about this.'..

'The White House and senior Congressional members,' the group wrote in an interim report released Tuesday, **'deliberately and knowingly pursued a policy that provided material support to terrorist organizations** in order to topple a ruler [Muammar Gaddafi] who had been working closely with the West actively to **suppress al-Qaeda.'**

'Some look at it as treason,' said Wayne Simmons, a former CIA officer who participated in the commission's research.

Pulitzer-prize winning investigative reporter Seymour Hersh – who broke the stories of the Mai Lai massacre in Vietnam and the Iraq prison torture scandals, which rightfully disgraced the Nixon and Bush administrations' war-fighting tactics – also reported[170] in 2014:

A highly classified annex to the report, not made public, described a secret agreement reached in early 2012 between the Obama and Erdoğan administrations. It pertained to the rat line. By the terms of the agreement, funding came from Turkey, as well as Saudi Arabia and Qatar; the CIA, with the support of MI6, was responsible for getting arms from Gaddafi's arsenals into Syria. A number of front companies were set up in Libya, some under the cover of Australian entities. Retired American soldiers, who didn't always know who was really employing them, were hired to manage procurement and shipping. The operation was run by David Petraeus, the CIA director who would soon resign when it became known he was having an affair with his biographer. (A spokesperson for Petraeus denied the operation ever took place.)

The operation had not been disclosed at the time it was set up to the congressional intelligence committees and the congressional leadership, as required by law since the 1970s. The involvement of MI6 enabled the CIA to evade the law by classifying the mission as a liaison operation. The former intelligence official explained that for years there has been a recognised exception in the law that permits the CIA not to report liaison activity to Congress, which would otherwise be owed a finding. (All proposed CIA covert operations must be described in a written document, known as a 'finding', submitted to the senior leadership of Congress for approval.) Distribution of the annex was limited to the staff aides who wrote the report and to the eight ranking members of Congress – the Democratic and Republican leaders of the House and Senate, and the Democratic and Republicans leaders on the House and Senate intelligence committees. This hardly constituted a genuine attempt at oversight: the eight leaders are not known to gather together to raise questions or discuss the secret information they receive.

The annex didn't tell the whole story of what happened in Benghazi before the attack, nor did it explain why the American consulate was attacked. **'The consulate's only mission was to provide cover for the moving of arms,' the former intelligence official, who has read the annex, said. 'It had no real political role.'**

Secret intelligence reports from 2011, written before and during the illegal US-led attack on Libya and recently obtained by the

Washington Times, state:[171] "There is a close link between al Qaeda, Jihadi organizations, and the opposition in Libya..."

Indeed, the Libyan rebel commander admitted[172] at the time that his fighters had links to Al Qaeda. And see this[173].

Iran

As noted by Seymour Hersh and others, the U.S. supports terrorists[174] within Iran. (See the next chapter "Born of the USA" by Wayne Madsen in this volume.)

Widespread Support for Terror

The director of the National Security Agency under Ronald Reagan – Lt. General William Odom said:[175] "**By any measure the US has long used terrorism**. In '78-79 the Senate was trying to pass a law against international terrorism – in every version they produced, the lawyers said the US would be in violation." (audio here[176]).

The Washington Post reported[177] in 2010: "The United States has long been an **exporter of terrorism**, according to a secret CIA analysis released Wednesday by the Web site WikiLeaks."[178]

Wikipedia notes[179]:

> Chomsky and Herman observed that terror was concentrated in the U.S. sphere of influence in the Third World, and documented terror carried out by U.S. client states in Latin America. They observed that of ten Latin American countries that had death squads, **all** were U.S. client states...
>
> They concluded that **the global rise in state terror was a result of U.S. foreign policy**...
>
> In 1991, a book edited by Alexander L. George [the Graham H. Stuart Professor of Political Science Emeritus at Stanford University] also argued that other Western powers sponsored terror in Third World countries. It concluded that **the U.S. and its allies were the main supporters of terrorism throughout the world**.

Indeed, the U.S. has created death squads in Latin America, Iraq and Syria[180].

Some in the American military have intentionally tried to "out-terrorize the terrorists"[181]. As Truthout notes[182]:

> Both [specialists Ethan McCord and Josh Stieber] say they saw their mission as a plan to "out-terrorize the terrorists," in order to make the general populace more afraid of the Americans than they were of insurgent groups. In the interview with [Scott] Horton, Horton pressed Stieber:

"... a fellow veteran of yours from the same battalion has said that you guys had a standard operating procedure, SOP, that said – and I guess this is a reaction to some EFP attacks on y'all's Humvees and stuff that killed some guys – that from now on if a roadside bomb goes off, IED goes off, everyone who survives the attack get out and fire in all directions at anybody who happens to be nearby ... that this was actually an order from above. Is that correct? Can you, you know, verify that?

Stieber answered:

"Yeah, it was an order that came from Kauzlarich himself, and it had the philosophy that, you know, as Finkel does describe in the book, that we were under pretty constant threat, and what he leaves out is the response to that threat. But the philosophy was that if each time one of these roadside bombs went off where you don't know who set it ... the way we were told to respond was to open fire on anyone in the area, with the philosophy that that would intimidate them, to be proactive in stopping people from making these bombs ..."

Terrorism is defined[183] as "The use of violence and threats to intimidate or coerce, especially for political purposes."

So McCord and Stieber are correct: this constitutes terrorism by American forces in Iraq.

False Flags

The U.S. and other "civilized" countries not only back terrorists, but sometimes carry out terrorist attacks themselves ... and falsely blame them on others.

Specifically, governments from around the world *admit* they've used the bully's trick ... attack first, and then blame the victim:

• Japanese troops set off a small explosion on a train track in 1931, and falsely blamed it on China in order to justify an invasion of Manchuria. This is known as[184] the "Mukden Incident" or the "Manchurian Incident". The Tokyo International Military Tribunal found[185]: "Several of the participators in the plan, including Hashimoto [a high-ranking Japanese army officer], *have on various occasions* admitted[186] their part in the plot and have stated that the object of the 'Incident' was to afford an excuse for the occupation of Manchuria by the Kwantung Army ...." And see this[187]

• A major with the Nazi SS admitted[188] at the Nuremberg trials that – under orders from the chief of the Gestapo – he and some other Nazi operatives faked attacks on their own people and resources which they blamed on the Poles, to justify the invasion of Poland. Nazi general Franz Halder also testified at the Nuremberg trials that Nazi leader

Hermann Goering admitted[189] to setting fire to the German parliament building in 1933, and then falsely blaming the communists for the arson

- Soviet leader Nikita Khrushchev admitted[190] in writing that the Soviet Union's Red Army shelled the Russian village of Mainila in 1939 – while blaming the attack on Finland – as a basis for launching the "Winter War" against Finland. Russian president Boris Yeltsin agreed[191] that Russia had been the aggressor in the Winter War

- The Russian Parliament admits[192] that Soviet leader Joseph Stalin ordered his secret police to execute 22,000 Polish army officers and civilians in 1940, and then blamed it on the Nazis. Current Russian president Putin and former Soviet leader Gorbachev have also admitted[193] that the Soviets were responsible for the massacre

- Israel admits[194] that an Israeli terrorist cell operating in Egypt planted bombs in several buildings, including U.S. diplomatic facilities, then left behind "evidence" implicating the Arabs as the culprits (one of the bombs detonated prematurely, allowing the Egyptians to identify the bombers, and several of the Israelis later confessed) (and see this[195] and this[196])

- The CIA admits[197] that it hired Iranians in the 1950's to pose as Communists and stage bombings in Iran in order to turn the country against its democratically-elected prime minister

- The Turkish Prime Minister admitted[198] that the Turkish government carried out the 1955 bombing on a Turkish consulate in Greece – also damaging the nearby birthplace of the founder of modern Turkey – and blamed it on Greece, for the purpose of inciting and justifying anti-Greek violence

- The British Prime Minister admitted[199] to his defense secretary that he and American president Dwight Eisenhower approved a plan in 1957 to carry out attacks in Syria and blame it on the Syrian government as a way to effect regime change

- The former Italian Prime Minister, an Italian judge, and the former head of Italian counterintelligence[200] admit that NATO, with the help of the Pentagon and CIA, carried out terror bombings in Italy and other European countries in the 1950s and blamed the communists, in order to rally people's support for their governments in Europe in their fight against communism[201]. As one participant in this formerly-secret program stated: "You had to attack civilians, people, women, children, innocent people, unknown people far removed from any political game. The reason was quite simple. They were supposed to force these people, the Italian public, to turn to the state to ask for greater security"[202] (and see this[203])(Italy and other European countries subject to the terror campaign had joined NATO before the bombings occurred). And watch this BBC special[204]. They also allegedly carried out terror attacks in France, Belgium, Denmark, Germany, Greece, the Netherlands, Norway, Portugal, the UK[205], and other countries

- In 1960, American Senator George Smathers suggested[206] that the U.S. launch "a false attack made on Guantanamo Bay which would give us the excuse of actually fomenting a fight which would then give us the excuse to go in and [overthrow Castro]".

- Official State Department documents show that, in 1961, the head of the Joint Chiefs and other high-level officials discussed[207] blowing up a consulate in the Dominican Republic in order to justify an invasion of that country. The plans were not carried out, but they were all discussed as serious proposals

- As admitted by the U.S. government, recently declassified documents show that in 1962, the American Joint Chiefs of Staff signed off on a plan to *blow up AMERICAN airplanes* (using an elaborate plan involving the switching of airplanes), and also to *commit terrorist acts on American soil*, and then to blame it on the Cubans in order to justify an invasion of Cuba. See the following ABC news report[208]; the official documents[209]; and watch this interview [210]with the former Washington Investigative Producer for ABC's World News Tonight with Peter Jennings.

- In 1963, the U.S. Department of Defense wrote a paper promoting[211] attacks on nations within the Organization of American States – such as Trinidad-Tobago or Jamaica – and then falsely blaming them on Cuba.

- The U.S. Department of Defense even suggested[212] covertly paying a person in the Castro government to attack the United States: "The only area remaining for consideration then would be to bribe one of Castro's subordinate commanders to initiate an attack on Guantanamo."

- The NSA admits[213] that it lied[214] about what really happened in the Gulf of Tonkin incident[215] in 1964 … manipulating data to make it look like North Vietnamese boats fired on a U.S. ship so as to create a false justification for the Vietnam war

- A U.S. Congressional committee admitted[216] that – as part of its "Cointelpro" campaign – the FBI had used many provocateurs in the 1950s through 1970s to carry out violent acts and falsely blame them on political activists

- A top[217] Turkish general admitted[218] that Turkish forces burned down a mosque on Cyprus in the 1970s and blamed it on their enemy. He explained[219]: "In Special War, certain *acts of sabotage are staged and blamed on the enemy* to increase public resistance. We did this on

Cyprus; we even burnt down a mosque." In response to the surprised correspondent's incredulous look the general said, "I am giving an example"

- The German government admitted[220] (and see this[221]) that, in 1978, the German secret service detonated a bomb in the outer wall of a prison and planted "escape tools" on a prisoner – a member of the Red Army Faction – which the secret service wished to frame the bombing on

- A Mossad agent says[222] that, in 1984, Mossad planted a radio transmitter in Gaddafi's compound in Tripoli, Libya which broadcast fake terrorist transmissions recorded by Mossad, in order to frame Gaddafi as a terrorist supporter. Ronald Reagan bombed Libya immediately thereafter.

- The South African Truth and Reconciliation Council found[223] that, in 1989, the Civil Cooperation Bureau (a covert branch of the South African Defense Force) approached an explosives expert and asked him "to participate in an operation aimed at discrediting the ANC [the African National Congress] by bombing the police vehicle of the investigating officer into the murder incident", thus framing the ANC for the bombing

- An Algerian diplomat and several officers in the Algerian army admit[224] that, in the 1990s, the Algerian army frequently massacred Algerian civilians and then blamed Islamic militants for the killings (and see this video[225]; and Agence France-Presse, 9/27/2002, French Court Dismisses Algerian Defamation Suit Against Author)

- An Indonesian fact-finding team investigated violent riots which occurred in 1998, and determined that "elements of the military had been involved in the riots, some of which were deliberately provoked[226]".

- Senior Russian Senior military and intelligence officers admit[227] that the KGB blew up Russian apartment buildings in 1999 and falsely blamed it on Chechens, in order to justify an invasion of Chechnya (and see this report[228] and this discussion[229])

- According to the Washington Post[230], Indonesian police admit that the Indonesian military killed American teachers in Papua in 2002 and blamed the murders on a Papuan separatist group in order to get that group listed as a terrorist organization.

- The well-respected former Indonesian president also admits[231] that the government probably had a role in the Bali bombings

- As reported by BBC[232], the New York Times[233], and Associated Press[234], Macedonian officials admit that the government murdered seven innocent immigrants in cold blood and pretended that they were Al

Qaeda soldiers attempting to assassinate Macedonian police, in order to join the "war on terror"

- Senior police officials in Genoa, Italy admitted[235] that – in July 2001, at the G8 summit in Genoa – planted two Molotov cocktails and faked the stabbing of a police officer, in order to justify a violent crackdown[236] against protesters

- Although the FBI now admits that the 2001 anthrax attacks were carried out by one or more U.S. government scientists, a senior FBI official says that the FBI was actually *told* to blame the Anthrax attacks on Al Qaeda by White House officials[237] (remember what the anthrax letters looked like[238]). Government officials also confirm that the white House tried to link the anthrax to Iraq[239] as a justification for regime change in that country

- Similarly, the U.S. falsely blamed Iraq[240] for playing a role in the 9/11 attacks – as shown by a memo from the defense secretary[241] – as one of the main justifications[242] for launching the Iraq war. Even after the 9/11 Commission admitted[243] that there was no connection, Dick Cheney said[244] that the evidence is "overwhelming" that al Qaeda had a relationship with Saddam Hussein's regime, that Cheney "probably" had information unavailable to the Commission, and that the media was not 'doing their homework' in reporting such ties. Top U.S. government officials now admit[245] that the Iraq war was really launched for oil … not 9/11 or weapons of mass destruction (despite previous "lone wolf" claims, many U.S. government officials now say[246] that 9/11 was state-sponsored terror; but Iraq was *not* the state which backed the hijackers)

- Former Department of Justice lawyer John Yoo suggested[247] in 2005 that the US should go on the offensive against al-Qaeda, having "our intelligence agencies create a false terrorist organization. It could have its own websites, recruitment centers, training camps, and fundraising operations. It could launch fake terrorist operations and claim credit for real terrorist strikes, helping to sow confusion within al-Qaeda's ranks, causing operatives to doubt others' identities and to question the validity of communications."

- United Press International reported[248] in June 2005:

  U.S. intelligence officers are reporting that some of the insurgents in Iraq are using recent-model Beretta 92 pistols, but the pistols seem to have had their serial numbers erased. The numbers do not appear to have been physically removed; the pistols seem to have come off a production line without any serial numbers. Analysts suggest the lack of serial numbers indicates that the weapons were intended for intelligence operations or terrorist cells with substantial government backing. Analysts speculate that these guns are probably from either Mossad or the CIA. Analysts speculate that agent provocateurs may be using the untraceable weapons even as U.S. authorities use insurgent attacks against civilians as evidence of the illegitimacy of the resistance.

- Undercover Israeli soldiers admitted[249] in 2005 to throwing stones at other Israeli soldiers so they could blame it on Palestinians, as an excuse to crack down on peaceful protests by the Palestinians

- Quebec police admitted[250] that, in 2007, thugs carrying rocks to a peaceful protest were actually undercover Quebec police officers (and see this[251])

- At the G20 protests in London in 2009, a British member of parliament saw[252] plain clothes police officers attempting to incite the crowd to violence

- Egyptian politicians admitted[253] (and see this[254]) that government employees looted priceless museum artifacts in 2011 to try to discredit the protesters

- A Colombian army colonel has admitted[255] that his unit murdered 57 civilians, then dressed them in uniforms and claimed they were rebels killed in combat

- U.S. soldiers have admitted[256] that if they kill innocent Iraqis and Afghanis, they then "drop" automatic weapons near their body so they can pretend they were militants.

- The highly-respected writer for the Telegraph Ambrose Evans-Pritchard says that the head of Saudi intelligence – Prince Bandar – recently admitted[257] that the Saudi government controls "Chechen" terrorists

- High-level American sources admitted[258] that the Turkish government – a fellow NATO country – carried out the chemical weapons attacks blamed on the Syrian government; and high-ranking Turkish government officials admitted[259] on tape plans to carry out attacks and blame it on the Syrian government

- The former Ukrainian security chief admits[260] that the sniper attacks which started the Ukrainian coup were carried out in order to frame others

- Britain's spy agency has admitted[261] (and see this[262]) that it carries out "digital false flag" attacks on targets, framing people[263] by writing offensive or unlawful material ... and blaming it on the target.

Part 4: What's the Real Story?

With the historical background in Parts 2 and 3, we can now look at the deeper story behind ISIS.

America's Closest Allies In the Mideast Support ISIS

America's top military official – the Chairman of the Joint Chiefs of Staff, General Martin E. Dempsey – and Senator Lindsey Graham admitted[264] last September in a Senate Armed Services Committee hearing that America's closest allies are supporting ISIS[265]:

> SEN. LINDSEY GRAHAM (R), SOUTH CAROLINA, MEMBER OF ARMED SERVICES COMMITTEE: Do you know any major Arab ally that embraces ISIL?
>
> GEN. MARTIN DEMPSEY, CHAIRMAN, JOINT CHIEFS OF STAFF: **I know major Arab allies who fund them**.
>
> GRAHAM: Yeah, but do they embrace them? **They fund them because the Free Syrian Army couldn't fight Assad. They were trying to beat Assad**. I think they realized the folly of their ways.

Four-Star General Wesley Clark – who served as the Supreme Allied Commander of NATO – agrees[266].

So does Vice President Joe Biden[267].

A German minister says[268] that U.S. ally Qatar funds ISIS.

ABC News reports:[269] "**The Sunni rebels [inside Syria] are supported by the Islamist rulers of Saudi Arabia, Qatar and Turkey, as well as the *U.S.*, France, Britain** and others."

The Independent headlines[270] "Iraq crisis: How **Saudi Arabia helped Isis** take over the north of the country":

> Some time before 9/11, Prince Bandar bin Sultan, once the powerful Saudi ambassador in Washington and head of Saudi intelligence until a few months ago, had a revealing and ominous conversation with the **head of the British Secret Intelligence Service, MI6, Sir Richard Dearlove**. Prince Bandar told him: "The time is not far off in the Middle East, Richard, when it will be literally 'God help the Shia'. More than a billion Sunnis have simply had enough of them."..
>
> There is no doubt about the accuracy of the quote by Prince Bandar, secretary-general of the Saudi National Security Council from 2005 and head of General Intelligence between 2012 and 2014, the crucial two years when al-Qa'ida-type jihadis took over the Sunni-armed opposition in Iraq and Syria. Speaking at the Royal United Services Institute last week, Dearlove, who headed MI6 from 1999 to 2004, emphasised the significance of Prince Bandar's words, saying that

they constituted "a chilling comment that I remember very well indeed".

He does not doubt that substantial and sustained funding from private donors in **Saudi Arabia and Qatar**, to which the authorities may have turned a blind eye, has played a central role in the Isis surge into Sunni areas of Iraq. He said: "**Such things simply do not happen spontaneously.**" This sounds realistic since the tribal and communal leadership in Sunni majority provinces is much beholden to Saudi and Gulf paymasters, and would be **unlikely to cooperate with Isis without their consent**...

Dearlove ... sees Saudi strategic thinking as being shaped by two deep-seated beliefs or attitudes. First, **they are convinced that there "can be no legitimate or admissible challenge to the Islamic purity of their Wahhabi credentials as guardians of Islam's holiest shrines"**. But, perhaps more significantly given the deepening Sunni-Shia confrontation, the Saudi belief that they possess a monopoly of Islamic truth leads them to be "deeply attracted towards any militancy which can effectively challenge Shia-dom".

Western governments traditionally play down the connection between Saudi Arabia and its Wahhabist faith, on the one hand, and jihadism, whether of the variety espoused by Osama bin Laden and al-Qa'ida or by Abu Bakr al-Baghdadi's Isis. There is nothing conspiratorial or secret about these links: 15 out of 19 of the 9/11 hijackers were Saudis, as was Bin Laden and most of the private donors who funded the operation...

But there has always been a second theme to Saudi policy towards al-Qa'ida type jihadis, contradicting Prince Bandar's approach and seeing jihadis as a mortal threat to the Kingdom. Dearlove illustrates this attitude by relating how, soon after 9/11, he visited the Saudi capital Riyadh with Tony Blair.

He remembers the then **head of Saudi General Intelligence "literally shouting at me across his office: '9/11 is a mere pinprick on the West**. In the medium term, it is nothing more than a series of personal tragedies. What these terrorists want is to destroy the House of Saud and remake the Middle East.'" In the event, **Saudi Arabia** adopted both policies, **encouraging the jihadis** as a useful tool of Saudi anti-Shia influence abroad but suppressing them at home as a threat to the status quo. It is this dual policy that has fallen apart over the last year.

Saudi sympathy for anti-Shia "militancy" is identified in leaked US official documents. The then US Secretary of State **Hillary Clinton wrote in December 2009 in a cable released by Wikileaks that**

"Saudi Arabia remains a critical financial support base for al-Qa'ida, the Taliban, LeT [Lashkar-e-Taiba in Pakistan] and other terrorist groups."..

Saudi Arabia and its allies are in practice playing into the hands of Isis which is swiftly gaining full control of the Sunni opposition in Syria and Iraq...

For all his gargantuan mistakes, Maliki's failings are not the reason why the Iraqi state is disintegrating. What destabilised Iraq from 2011 on was the revolt of the Sunni in Syria and the takeover of that revolt by jihadis, who were often **sponsored by donors in Saudi Arabia, Qatar, Kuwait and United Arab Emirates**. Again and again Iraqi politicians warned that by not seeking to close down the civil war in Syria, Western leaders were making it inevitable that the conflict in Iraq would restart. "I guess they just didn't believe us and were fixated on getting rid of [President Bashar al-] Assad," said an Iraqi leader in Baghdad last week. Of course, US and British politicians and diplomats would argue that they were in no position to bring an end to the Syrian conflict. But this is misleading. By insisting that peace negotiations must be about the departure of Assad from power, something that was never going to happen since Assad held most of the cities in the country and his troops were advancing, the US and Britain made sure the war would continue...

Saudi Arabia has created a Frankenstein's monster over which it is rapidly losing control. **The same is true of its allies such as Turkey which has been a vital back-base for Isis** and Jabhat al-Nusra by keeping the 510-mile-long Turkish-Syrian border open.

The Daily Beast (a media company formerly owned by Newsweek[271]) notes[272], in a story entitled "America's Allies Are Funding ISIS":

The Islamic State of Iraq and Syria (ISIS), now threatening Baghdad, was funded for years by wealthy donors in Kuwait, Qatar, and Saudi Arabia, three U.S. allies that have dual agendas in the war on terror...

The extremist group that is threatening the existence of the Iraqi state was built and grown for years with the help of elite donors from **American supposed allies in the Persian Gulf region**...

A key component of ISIS's support came from wealthy individuals in the Arab Gulf States of Kuwait, Qatar and Saudi Arabia. Sometimes the support came with the **tacit nod of approval from those regimes** ....

Gulf donors support ISIS, the Syrian branch of al Qaeda called the al Nusrah Front, and other Islamic groups fighting on the ground in Syria ....

Donors in Kuwait, the Sunni majority Kingdom on Iraq's border, have taken advantage of Kuwait's weak financial rules to channel hundreds of millions of dollars to a host of Syrian rebel brigades, according to a December 2013 report by The Brookings Institution, a Washington think tank that receives some funding from the Qatari government...

"The U.S. Treasury is aware of this activity and has expressed concern about this flow of private financing. But Western diplomats' and officials' general response has been a collective shrug," the report states.

When confronted with the problem, Gulf leaders often justify allowing their Salafi constituents to fund Syrian extremist groups ....

That's what Prince Bandar bin Sultan, head of Saudi intelligence since 2012 and former Saudi ambassador in Washington, reportedly told Secretary of State John Kerry[273] when Kerry pressed him on Saudi financing of extremist groups earlier this year. Saudi Arabia has retaken a leadership role in past months guiding help to the Syrian armed rebels, displacing Qatar, which was seen as supporting some of the worst of the worst organizations on the ground.

Business Insider notes[274]:

The Islamic State for Iraq and the Levant ... is also receiving private donations from wealthy Sunnis in **American-allied Gulf nations such as Kuwait, Qatar, and, possibly, Saudi Arabia**...

As far back as March[275], Iraqi Prime Minister Nouri al-Maliki has accused Saudi Arabia and Qatar of openly funding ISIS as his troops were fighting them.

"I accuse them of inciting and encouraging the terrorist movements. I accuse them of supporting them politically and in the media, of supporting them with money and by buying weapons for them," he told France 24 television.

In Kuwait, donors have taken advantage of weak terror financing control laws to funnel hundreds of millions of dollars to various Syrian rebel groups, including ISIS, according to a December 2013 report[276] by The Brookings Institution, which receives some funding from the government of Qatar.

"Over the last two and a half years, Kuwait has emerged as a financing and organizational hub for charities and individuals supporting Syria's myriad rebel groups," the report said, adding that money from donors in other gulf nations is collected in Kuwait before traveling through Turkey or Jordan to reach the insurgents...

Ironically, Kuwait is a staging area for individuals funneling money to an ISIS organization that is aligned with whatever is left of the

Baathist regime once led by Saddam Hussein[277]. In 1990, the U.S. went to war with Iraq over Hussein's invasion and occupation of Kuwait.

Turkey Supports ISIS

NATO member Turkey has long been directly supporting ISIS[278].

The Jerusalem Post reports that an ISIS fighter says that Turkey funds the terrorist group[279].

A German news program – with English subtitles – shows that Turkey is sending terrorists into Syria: Opposition Turkish lawmakers say that the government is protecting and cooperating with ISIS and Al Qaeda terrorists[280], and providing free medical care to their leaders.

According to a leading Turkish newspaper (Today's Zaman), Turkish nurses are sick of providing free medical treatment to ISIS terrorists[281] in Turkish hospitals.

Now, Turkey is massively bombing the most effective on-the-ground fighters against ISIS. As Time Magazine pointed out[282] in June 2015:

> Ethnic Kurds—who on Tuesday scored their second and third significant victories over ISIS in the space of eight days—are **by far the most effective force fighting ISIS** in both Iraq and Syria.

And yet Turkey is trying to destroy the Kurds. Time writes[283]:

> Since [Turkey announced that it was joining the war against ISIS] it has arrested more than 1,000 people in Turkey and carried out waves of air raids in neighboring Syria and Iraq. But **most of those arrests and air strikes**, say Kurdish leaders, **have hit Kurdish and left wing groups, not ISIS**.

Turkey is also supporting ISIS by buying its oil ... its main source of funding. The Guardian reported[284]:

> US special forces raided the compound of an Islamic State[285] leader in eastern Syria in May, they made sure not to tell the neighbours.
>
> The target of that raid, the first of its kind since US jets returned to the skies over Iraq last August, was an Isis official responsible for oil smuggling, named Abu Sayyaf[286]. He was almost unheard of outside the upper echelons of the terror group, but he was well known to Turkey. From mid-2013, the Tunisian fighter had been responsible for smuggling oil from Syria's eastern fields, which the group had by then commandeered. Black market oil quickly became the main driver of Isis revenues – and Turkish buyers were its **main clients**.

As a result, the oil trade between the jihadis and the Turks was held up as evidence of an alliance between the two...

In the wake of the raid that killed Abu Sayyaf, suspicions of an undeclared alliance have hardened. One **senior western official** familiar with the intelligence gathered at the slain leader's compound said that direct dealings between Turkish officials and ranking Isis members was now **"undeniable"**.

"There are hundreds of flash drives and documents that were seized there," the official told the *Observer*. "They are being analysed at the moment, but the links are already so clear that they could end up having profound policy implications for the relationship between us and Ankara."..

However, Turkey has openly supported other jihadi groups, such as Ahrar al-Sham[287], which espouses much of al-Qaida's ideology, and Jabhat al-Nusra, which is proscribed as a terror organisation by much of the US and Europe. "The distinctions they draw [with other opposition groups] are thin indeed," said the western official. "There is no doubt at all that they militarily cooperate with both."..

One Isis member says the organisation remains a long way from establishing a self-sustaining economy across the area of Syria and Iraq it controls. "They need the Turks. I know of a lot of cooperation and it scares me," he said. "I don't see how Turkey can attack the organisation too hard. There are shared interests."

While the Guardian is one of Britain's leading newspapers, many in the alternative press have long[288] pointed[289] out[290] Turkey's support for ISIS.

And experts[291], Kurds[292], and Vice President Joe Biden[293] have accused Turkey of enabling ISIS.

Israel Supports ISIS

The Israeli air force has bombed[294] near the Syrian capital of Damascus, and attacked agricultural facilities and warehouses (the Syrian government is the other main opponent of ISIS in Syria besides the Kurds).

The Israeli military recently admitted[295] supporting Syrian jihadis. Specifically, the Times of Israel reported[296] in June 2015:

> **Defense Minister Moshe Ya'alon said Monday that Israel has been providing aid to Syrian rebels**, thus keeping the Druze in Syria out of immediate danger. Israeli officials have previously balked at confirming on the record that the country has been helping forces that are fighting to overthrow Syrian President Bashar Assad...

"We've assisted them under two conditions," Ya'alon said of the Israeli medical aid to the Syrian rebels, **some of whom are presumably fighting with al-Qaeda affiliate al-Nusra Front** to topple Syrian President Bashar Assad. "That they don't get too close to the border, and that they don't touch the Druze."

(Al Nusra **is** Al Qaeda, and closely affiliated with ISIS[297].)

The Times of Israel reported[298] in 2014:

A Free Syrian Army commander, arrested last month by the Islamist militia Al-Nusra Front, told his captors he collaborated with Israel in return for medical and military support, in a video released this week.

In a video[299] uploaded to YouTube Monday ... Sharif As-Safouri, the commander of the Free Syrian Army's Al-Haramein Battalion, admitted to having entered Israel five times to meet with Israeli officers who later provided him with Soviet anti-tank weapons and light arms. Safouri was abducted by the al-Qaeda-affiliated Al-Nusra Front[300] in the Quneitra area, near the Israeli border, on July 22.

"The [opposition] factions would receive support and send the injured in [to Israel] on condition that the Israeli fence area is secured. No person was allowed to come near the fence without prior coordination with Israel authorities," Safouri said in the video...

In the edited confession video, in which Safouri seems physically unharmed, he says that at first he met with an Israeli officer named Ashraf at the border and was given an Israeli cellular phone. He later met with another officer named Younis and with the two men's commander, Abu Daoud. In total, Safouri said he entered Israel five times for meetings that took place in Tiberias.

Following the meetings, Israel began providing Safouri and his men with "basic medical support and clothes" as well as weapons, which included 30 Russian [rifles], 10 RPG launchers with 47 rockets, and 48,000 5.56 millimeter bullets.

Haaretz reported[301] the same year:

The Syrian opposition is willing to give up claims to the Golan Heights in return for cash and Israeli military aid against President Bashar Assad, a top opposition official told Al Arab newspaper, according to a report in Al Alam...

The Western-backed militant groups want Israel to enforce a no-fly zone over parts of southern Syria to protect rebel bases from air strikes by Assad's forces, according to the report.

In a separate article, Haaretz also noted[302]:

According to reports, Israel has also been involved, and even provided active assistance in at least one attack by rebel troops four months ago, when its communications and intelligence base on Mount Hermon jammed the Syrian army's communications system and the information relayed between its fighting forces and their headquarters.

Jacky Hugi – an Arab affairs analyst for Israeli army radio – recently wrote[303]:

> The Israeli security establishment should gradually abandon its **emerging alliance[304] with the Syrian rebels** .....
>
> It is a dangerous, irresponsible gamble to choose Assad's enemies[305] and encourage his collapse — it would be playing with fire.

The U.S. Supports ISIS

Former CIA boss and 4-star general David Petraeus – who still (believe it or not) holds a lot of sway in Washington – suggests[306] we should arm Al Qaeda. Quite a few mainstream Americans are also saying[307] we should support Al Qaeda in Iraq and Syria.

Influential New York Times columnist Thomas Friedman asks[308] if we should arm *ISIS* itself, so as to counter Iranian influence. This isn't just empty rhetoric.

A former Al Qaeda commander says[309] that ISIS *already* works for the CIA.

Former FBI translator Sibel Edmonds – deemed credible by the Department of Justice's Inspector General, several senators[310] (free subscription required), and a coalition of prominent conservative and liberal groups[311] – says[312] that the CIA and NATO started recruiting and training people at a NATO base in Turkey – right near the Syrian border – to stage terrorist attacks in Syria to overthrow the Syrian government ... and that this was the *birth* of ISIS:

> In 2011, months and months before Syria came in the headlines – anything about Syria was written on the New York Times, Washington Post and CNN – we broke a story [background here[313], here[314], here[315] and here[316]] based on my sources here in United States military but also in Turkey about the fact that special **CIA/NATO forces in a NATO base in Turkey**, which is in the southern portion of Turkey **very close to the Syrian border**, they were bringing in, in Turkey, **the CIA/NATO Gladio unit, they were recruiting and bringing in people from northern Syria into these camps, part of the US air force base in southern Turkey. They were training them – military training – they were arming them, and they were basically directing them towards create terror events inside Syria, not only against Assad, but also in various villages and regions against the people, against public...**

That was the training and beginning of the ISIS brand. It started as ISIL and then turned to ISIS and now for short IS. This was completed by design, it was created and the people who are part of the so called ISIS they were carefully selected, brought into the U.S. NATO base in Turkey, they were trained they were funneled, and this is what they were told to do. They created a new brand and a new brand with purpose of replacing the old brand: Al Qaeda.

Sound like a conspiracy theory?

Unfortunately, an internal U.S. Defense Intelligence Agency (DIA) document produced recently shows that the U.S. knew that the actions of "the West, Gulf countries and Turkey" in Syria might create a terrorist group like ISIS and an Islamic caliphate[317].

By way of background, a non-profit organization called Judicial Watch has – for many years – obtained sensitive U.S. government documents through freedom of information requests and lawsuits. The government just produced documents[318] to Judicial Watch in response to a freedom of information suit which show that the West has long supported ISIS.

The documents were written by the U.S. Defense Intelligence Agency (DIA) on August 12, 2012 ... years *before*[319] ISIS burst onto the world stage. Here are excerpts from the documents (our emphasis on the relevant parts):

A. INTERNALLY, EVENTS ARE TAKING A CLEAR SECTARIAN DIRECTION.

B. THE SALAFIST, THE MUSLIM BROTHERHOOD, AND AQI ARE THE MAJOR FORCES DRIVING THE INSURGENCY IN SYRIA.

C. THE WEST, GULF COUNTRIES, AND TURKEY SUPPORT THE OPPOSITION; WHILE RUSSIA, CHINA. AND IRAN SUPPORT THE REGIME.

Why is this important? It shows that extreme Muslim terrorists – salafists[320], Muslim Brotherhood, and AQI (i.e. Al Qaeda in Iraq) – have *always* been the "major forces driving the insurgency in Syria."

This verifies what the alternative media has been saying for years: there *aren't any* moderate rebels[321] in Syria (and see this[322], this[323] and this[324]).

Moreover, the newly-declassified document continues:

TRAIN THEM ON THE IRAQI SIDE, IN ADDITION TO HARBORING REFUGEES (SYRIA).

C. IF THE SITUATION UNRAVELS THERE IS THE POSSIBILITY OF ESTABLISHING A DECLARED OR UNDECLARED SALAFIST PRINCIPALITY IN EASTERN SYRIA (HASAKA AND DER ZOR),

AND THIS IS EXACTLY WHAT THE SUPPORTING POWERS TO THE OPPOSITION WANT, IN ORDER TO ISOLATE THE SYRIAN REGIME, WHICH IS CONSIDERED THE STRATEGIC DEPTH OF THE SHIA EXPANSION (IRAQ AND IRAN).

D. THE DETERIORATION OF THE SITUATION HAS DIRE CONSEQUENCES ON THE IRAQI SITUATION AND ARE AS FOLLOWS;

-1. THIS CREATES THE IDEAL ATMOSPHERE FOR AQI TO RETURN TO ITS OLD POCKETS IN MOSUL AND RAMADI AND WILL PROVIDE A RENEWED MOMENTUM UNDER THE PRESUMPTION OF UNIFYING THE JIHAD AMONG SUNNI IRAQ AND SYRIA, AND THE REST OF THE SUNNIS IN THE ARAB WORLD AGAINST WHAT IT CONSIDERS ONE ENEMY, THE DISSENTERS. ISI COULD ALSO DECLARE AN ISLAMIC STATE THROUGH ITS UNION WITH OTHER TERRORIST ORGANIZATIONS IN IRAQ AND SYRIA, WHICH WILL CREATE GRAVE DANGER IN REGARDS TO UNIFYING IRAQ AND THE PROTECTION OF ITS TERRITORY.

Yes, you read that correctly:

> …**there is the possibility of establishing a declared or undeclared Salafist Principality in eastern Syria** (Hasaka and Der Zor), **and this is exactly what the supporting powers to the opposition want**, in order to isolate the Syrian regime ….

In other words, the powers supporting the Syrian opposition – the West, our Gulf allies, and Turkey *wanted* an Islamic caliphate in order to challenge Syrian president Assad.

This is a big deal. A former British Army and Metropolitan Police counter-terrorism intelligence officer and a former MI5 officer confirm[325] that the newly-released documents are a smoking gun.

And the former **head** of the DIA – Lieutenant General Michael Flynn – confirmed its importance as well. By any measure, Flynn was a top-level American military commander. Flynn served as[326]:

- The Director of the U.S. Intelligence Agency
- The Director of intelligence for Joint Special Operations Command (JSOC), the main military agency responsible for targeting Al-Qaeda and other Islamic terrorists
- The Commander of the Joint Functional Component Command for Intelligence, Surveillance and Reconnaissance
- The Chair of the Military Intelligence Board
- Assistant director of national intelligence

Flynn confirmed[327] the authenticity of the document in a subsequent interview, and said:

[Interviewer] So the administration turned a blind eye to your analysis?

[Flynn] **I don't know that they turned a blind eye, I think it was a decision. I think it was a willful decision**.

[Interviewer] A willful decision to support an insurgency that had Salafists, Al Qaeda and the Muslim Brotherhood?

[Flynn] It was a **willful decision** *to do what they're doing.*

NBC News[328], the Wall Street Journal[329], CNN[330] and others report that the U.S. has committed to provide air power to support Muslim jihadis in Syria.

World Net Daily reports that the U.S. trained Islamic jihadis – who would later join ISIS [331]– in Jordan.

Der Spiegel and the Guardian confirmed[332] that the U.S., France and England trained hundreds if not *thousands* of Islamic fighters in Jordan.

POSTSCRIPT:

ISIS does not represent mainstream Islam.

For example, the Intercept points out that ISIS has "more in common with Mao's Red Guards or the Khmer Rouge than it does with the Muslim empires of antiquity[333]".

Huffington Post reports[334]:

> Can you guess which books the wannabe jihadists Yusuf Sarwar and Mohammed Ahmed ordered online from Amazon before they set out from Birmingham to fight in Syria last May? A copy of *Milestones* by the Egyptian Islamist Sayyid Qutb? No. How about *Messages to the World: the Statements of Osama Bin Laden*? Guess again. Wait, *The Anarchist Cookbook*, right? Wrong.
>
> Sarwar and Ahmed, both of whom pleaded guilty to terrorism offences last month, purchased **Islam for Dummies and The Koran for Dummies**. You could not ask for better evidence to bolster the argument that the 1,400-year-old Islamic faith has little to do with the modern jihadist movement. The swivel-eyed young men who take sadistic pleasure in bombings and beheadings may try to justify their violence with recourse to religious rhetoric – think the killers of Lee Rigby screaming "Allahu Akbar" at their trial; think of Islamic State beheading the photojournalist James Foley as part of its "holy war" – but religious fervour isn't what motivates most of them.

In 2008, a classified briefing note on radicalisation, prepared by MI5's behavioural science unit, was leaked to the *Guardian*. It revealed that, "far from being religious zealots, a large number of those involved in terrorism do not practise their faith regularly. Many lack religious literacy and could . . . be regarded as religious novices." The analysts concluded that "a well-established religious identity **actually protects against violent radicalisation**", the newspaper said. [Here's the Guardian report[335].]

For more evidence, read the books of the forensic psychiatrist and former CIA officer Marc Sageman; the political scientist Robert Pape [Pape found that foreign occupation – and not religion[336] – made certain Arabs into terrorists; the CIA's top Bin Laden hunter agreed[337]]; the international relations scholar Rik Coolsaet; the Islamism expert Olivier Roy; the anthropologist Scott Atran. They have all studied the lives and backgrounds of hundreds of gun-toting, bomb-throwing jihadists and they all agree that Islam isn't to blame for the behaviour of such men (and, yes, they usually are men).

Instead they point to other drivers of radicalisation ....

When he lived in the Philippines in the 1990s, Khalid Sheikh Mohammed, described as "the principal architect" of the 11 September attacks by the 9/11 Commission, once flew a helicopter past a girlfriend's office building with a banner saying "I love you". His nephew Ramzi Yousef, sentenced to life in prison for his role in the 1993 World Trade Center bombing, also had a girlfriend and, like his uncle, was often spotted in Manila's red-light district. **The FBI agent who hunted Yousef said that he "hid behind a cloak of Islam".** Eyewitness accounts suggest the 9/11 hijackers were visiting bars and strip clubs in Florida and Las Vegas in the run-up to the attacks. The Spanish neighbours of Hamid Ahmidan, convicted for his role in the Madrid train bombings of 2004, remember him "zooming by on a motorcycle with his long-haired girlfriend, a Spanish woman with a taste for revealing outfits", according to press reports.

No wonder Muslim leaders worldwide condemn ISIS[338].

Similarly, the 9/11 hijackers used cocaine and drank alcohol, slept with prostitutes and attended strip clubs ... but they *did not worship at any mosque*. See this[339], this[340], this[341], this[342], this[343], this[344], this[345] and this[346].

As such, Islamic terrorists do not represent Muslims as a whole.

Endnotes

1. noted: http://www.youtube.com/watch?v=2a01Rg2g2Z8?start=745&end=761
2. themselves credit: http://www.washingtonsblog.com/2014/08/isis-terrorists-credit-iraq-war-success.html
3. reports: http://www.newyorker.com/magazine/2014/09/29/fight-lives
4. led to the rise of ISIS: http://www.washingtonsblog.com/2014/12/u-s-torture-program-created-isis.html
5. Guantanamo prison inspired ISIS atrocities: http://www.washingtonsblog.com/2015/02/guantanamo-inspires-isis-atrocities.html
6. wasn't even in Iraq: http://crooksandliars.com/cernig/bush-admits-al-qaeda-wasnt-iraq-invasion-so
7. admitted: http://abcnews.go.com/Politics/BushLegacy/story?id=6460837
8. captured American weapons leftover from the Iraq war: http://www.washingtonsblog.com/2014/07/isis-taking-iraq-using-captured-american-weapons.html
9. reports: http://www.dailystar.com.lb/News/Lebanon-News/2014/Sep-08/269883-frustration-drives-arsals-fsa-into-isis-ranks.ashx#ixzz3CpSZVuEG
10. Nusra Front [another extremist and hard-line Islamic terrorist group] :
11. non-aggression pact: https://now.mmedia.me/lb/en/nowsyrialatestnews/563491-syria-rebels-is-in-non-aggression-pact-near-damascus
12. with ISIS: http://www.middleeasteye.net/news/syria-1651994714
13. writes: http://www.nytimes.com/2014/09/12/world/middleeast/us-pins-hope-on-syrian-rebels-with-loyalties-all-over-the-map.html
14. Wall Street Journal: http://www.wsj.com/news/articles/SB10001424052702304626304579509401865454762
15. PBS: http://www.pbs.org/wgbh/pages/frontline/foreign-affairs-defense/syria-arming-the-rebels/syrian-rebels-describe-u-s-backed-training-in-qatar/
16. CNN: http://www.cnn.com/2013/09/12/politics/syria-arming-rebels/
17. New York Times: http://www.nytimes.com/2012/06/21/world/middleeast/cia-said-to-aid-in-steering-arms-to-syrian-rebels.html?_r=0
18. Medium: https://medium.com/dan-sanchez/where-does-isis-get-those-wonderful-toys-77cea955731a
19. Pulitzer prize-winning reporter Seymour Hersh: http://www.washingtonsblog.com/2014/04/real-benghazi-story.html
20. arming rebels rarely works: http://www.washingtonsblog.com/2014/10/cia-study-funding-rebels-rarely-works.html
21. reported: http://www.nytimes.com/2013/04/28/world/middleeast/islamist-rebels-gains-in-syria-create-dilemma-for-us.html?pagewanted=all&_r=0
22. warned: http://www.huffingtonpost.com/michael-shank/how-arming-syrian-rebels_b_3689592.html
23. committees' about-face decision last week: http://rt.com/usa/joint-chiefs-us-options-syria-445/
24. reject negotiation altogether: https://www.fas.org/sgp/crs/mideast/RL33487.pdf

25. 5 years before the civil war started ... and started arming them 4 years beforehand: http://www.washingtonsblog.com/2013/08/u-s-started-backing-syrian-opposition-years-before-the-uprising-started.html

26. discussed:
http://www.youtube.com/watch?v=W3HWiydFlJc?start=340&end=485

27. humanitarian reasons: http://www.washingtonsblog.com/2015/03/original-sin-first-humanitarian-war.html

28. summarized: http://www.washingtonsblog.com/2014/05/america-switched-sides-now-backs-al-qaeda-nazis.html

29. mainly Al Qaeda, and the U.S. has been supporting these terrorists:
http://www.washingtonsblog.com/2013/09/syrian-rebels-slit-throat-of-christian-man-who-refused-to-convert-to-islam-taunt-fiance-jesus-didnt-come-to-save-him.html

30. Wall Street Journal:
http://online.wsj.com/news/articles/SB10001424052702304431104579547183675484314

31. the National: http://www.thenational.ae/world/middle-east/al-qaeda-expands-influence-in-syrias-southern-front

32. Burned:
http://www.youtube.com/watch?feature=player_embedded&v=BZui1YVCVTY

33. flags:
http://www.youtube.com/watch?feature=player_embedded&v=R5OtSNDz6lU

34. Threatened to attack America:
http://www.washingtontimes.com/news/2013/sep/6/facebook-flap-syrian-rebels-post-image-selves-burn/

35. "When we finish with Assad, we will fight the U.S.!" :
http://www.mcclatchydc.com/2012/12/02/176123/al-qaida-linked-group-syria-rebels.html#storylink=cpy

36. won't finish until this [Al Qaeda] banner will be raised on top of the White House: http://www.infowars.com/fsa-rebel-we-wont-stop-until-al-qaeda-flag-raised-over-white-house/

37. "9/11 ideology":
http://www.israelnationalnews.com/News/News.aspx/175001#.U20gCaKaXYA

38. singing Bin Laden's praises:
http://www.thestudentroom.co.uk/showthread.php?t=2665274

39. celebrating the 9/11 attack: http://www.youtube.com/watch?v=vsq5ZRir-0k

40. reports: http://www.cbsnews.com/8301-202_162-57602799/al-qaeda-boss-ayman-al-zawahri-marks-9-11-with-call-for-more-attacks-on-u.s-soil/

41. are Al Qaeda: http://www.washingtonsblog.com/2013/09/kerry-we-have-to-send-terrorists-into-syria-to-make-sure-that-chemical-weapons-dont-fall-into-the-hands-of-terrorists.html

42. designated these guys as terrorists:
http://www.aljazeera.com/news/middleeast/2012/12/2012121117048117723.html

43. gaining more and more power:
http://worldnews.nbcnews.com/_news/2013/09/11/20438772-jihadis-gain-ground-in-syrian-rebel-movement-as-moderates-grow-desperate?lite

44. ending up in the hands of Al Qaeda:
http://www.nytimes.com/2012/10/15/world/middleeast/jihadists-receiving-most-arms-sent-to-syrian-rebels.html?pagewanted=all&_r=0
45. have chemical weapons: http://www.washingtonsblog.com/2013/09/classified-u-s-military-document-syrian-rebels-do-have-chemical-weapons.html
46. tripled the size of its territory in Syria:
http://www.washingtonsblog.com/2015/01/islamic-state-tripled-territory-syria-u-s-started-airstrikes.html
47. greatly expanded its territory in Iraq:
http://www.washingtonsblog.com/2015/05/in-iraq-isis-is-winning-and-the-united-states-is-losing.html
48. even more of Syria:
http://static3.businessinsider.com/image/55eec098bd86ef15008b88be-1944-1716/2000px-syria15.png
49. reported: http://www.nytimes.com/2007/07/18/world/africa/18iht-iraq.4.6718200.html?_r=4&
50. arrested in 2007:
http://web.archive.org/web/20070314153618/http://www.cnn.com/2007/WORLD/meast/03/09/iraq.main/index.html?eref=rss_latest
51. killed in 2007: http://edition.cnn.com/2007/WORLD/meast/05/03/iraq.main/
52. arrested again: http://www.huffingtonpost.com/2009/04/23/baghdad-suicide-bomber-ki_0_n_190455.html
53. killed again: http://www.reuters.com/article/2010/04/19/us-iraq-violence-alqaeda-idUSTRE63I3CL20100419
54. declared dead: http://www.nbcnews.com/id/4446084/ns/world_news-mideast_n_africa/t/iraq-militants-claim-al-zarqawi-dead/
55. said to be arrested: http://www.cbsnews.com/news/official-al-zarqawi-caught-freed/
56. several different times: http://www.chinadaily.com.cn/english/doc/2005-01/04/content_405831.htm
57. in 2006: http://www.cbsnews.com/news/whats-next-after-zarqawis-death/
58. cites: http://www.independent.co.uk/news/media/how-the-spooks-took-over-the-news-780672.html
59. reported: http://www.washingtonpost.com/wp-dyn/content/article/2006/04/09/AR2006040900890_pf.html
60. reported: http://www.youtube.com/watch?v=d-LbGW-8vig?start=625&end=751
61. explains: https://en.wikipedia.org/wiki/Mosul%E2%80%93Haifa_oil_pipeline
62. Background: http://en.wikipedia.org/wiki/Haifa#British_Mandate
63. reported: http://www.haaretz.com/print-edition/news/u-s-checking-possibility-of-pumping-oil-from-northern-iraq-to-haifa-via-jordan-1.98134
64. call: http://en.wikipedia.org/wiki/1948_Arab%E2%80%93Israeli_War
65. poison the Iraqi leader:
http://en.wikipedia.org/wiki/CIA_activities_in_Iraq#Iraq_1960
66. backed the coup which succeeded:
http://en.wikipedia.org/wiki/CIA_activities_in_Iraq#Iraq_1963
67. in 1991: http://www.washingtonsblog.com/2011/11/neoconservatives-planned-regime-change-throughout-the-middle-east-and-northern-africa-20-years-ago.html

68. admitted the war was about oil: http://www.washingtonsblog.com/2013/03/top-republican-leaders-say-iraq-war-was-really-for-oil.html
69. said: http://discussion.guardian.co.uk/comment-permalink/22064968
70. said: http://www.youtube.com/watch?v=9sd2JseupXQ?start=1305
71. said:
http://web.archive.org/web/20110715222651/http://www.timesonline.co.uk/tol/news/world/article2461214.ece
72. said:
http://www.boston.com/news/nation/articles/2005/08/31/bush_gives_new_reason_for_iraq_war/
73. said: http://firstread.nbcnews.com/_news/2008/05/02/4431009-mccain-iraq-war-was-for-oil
74. said: http://www.businessweek.com/stories/2008-08-29/bartiromo-talks-with-sarah-palinbusinessweek-business-news-stock-market-and-financial-advice
75. writes: http://www.thedailybeast.com/newsweek/2013/03/18/the-speechwriter-inside-the-bush-administration-during-the-iraq-war.html
76. politician and oil minister: http://en.wikipedia.org/wiki/Ahmed_Chalabi
77. said: http://www.youtube.com/watch?v=uFbpKKOEnAE
78. said: http://www.youtube.com/watch?v=G1p_tFnKqMA
79. Cheney and the U.S. oil chiefs planned the Iraq war before 9/11 in order to get control of its oil: http://www.washingtonsblog.com/2008/07/did-cheney-and-the-oil-bigs-plan-the-iraq-war-before-911.html
80. reported:
http://web.archive.org/web/20030402124132/http://www.sundayherald.com/28224
81. reported: http://www.independent.co.uk/news/uk/politics/secret-memos-expose-link-between-oil-firms-and-invasion-of-iraq-2269610.html
82. in order to calm oil markets:
http://en.wikipedia.org/wiki/1990_oil_price_shock#Iraqi_invasion_of_Kuwait_and_ensuing_economic_effects
83. quoted: http://content.time.com/time/magazine/0,9263,7601900820,00.html
84. in 1949:
http://en.wikipedia.org/wiki/March_1949_Syrian_coup_d%27%C3%A9tat
85. notes: http://coat.ncf.ca/our_magazine/links/issue51/articles/51_12-13.pdf
86. reports:
http://m.guardian.co.uk/politics/2003/sep/27/uk.syria1?cat=politics&type=article
87. vaguely familiar: http://en.wikipedia.org/wiki/Free_Syrian_Army
88. Shia Muslim sect: http://en.wikipedia.org/wiki/Druze
89. in 1991: http://www.washingtonsblog.com/2011/11/neoconservatives-planned-regime-change-throughout-the-middle-east-and-northern-africa-20-years-ago.html
90. reported: http://www.theguardian.com/environment/earth-insight/2013/aug/30/syria-chemical-attack-war-intervention-oil-gas-energy-pipelines
91. Roland Dumas: http://www.youtube.com/watch?v=jeyRwFHR8WY
92. private intelligence firm Stratfor: http://blogs.channel4.com/alex-thomsons-view/syria-spooks-wikileaks-military/5502
93. a meeting with Pentagon officials:
https://wikileaks.org/gifiles/docs/1671459_insight-military-intervention-in-syria-post-withdrawal.html

94. refused to sign:
http://www.google.com/hostednews/afp/article/ALeqM5jhPTvibpnk98IR09Amuc5
QzWQsIQ?docId=CNG.c0b07c0fd43690568ae07ab83f87f608.6d1
95. run a pipeline from the latter's North field:
http://www.thenational.ae/business/energy/qatar-seeks-gas-pipeline-to-turkey
96. an alternative $10 billion pipeline plan with Iran:
http://www.aljazeera.com/indepth/opinion/2012/08/201285133440424621.html
97. framework agreement for construction of the gas pipelines:
http://www.alarabiya.net/articles/2013/02/20/267257.html
98. direct slap in the face: http://oilprice.com/Geopolitics/Middle-East/IRAN-
IRAQ-Pipeline-to-Syria-Ups-Ante-in-Proxy-War-with-Qatar.html
99. "completely" in Saudi Arabia's hands:
http://www.google.com/hostednews/afp/article/ALeqM5jhPTvibpnk98IR09Amuc5
QzWQsIQ?docId=CNG.c0b07c0fd43690568ae07ab83f87f608.6d1
100. play ball: http://www.lawfareblog.com/2013/08/general-dempsey-on-syria-
intervention/
101. many other governments, as well: http://www.washingtonsblog.com/2014/09/u-
s-already-completed-regime-change-syria-iran-iraq-twice-oil-rich-countries.html
102. noted: http://www.ibtimes.com/syrian-oil-gas-little-known-facts-syrias-energy-
resources-russias-help-1402405
103. key chess piece: http://www.washingtonsblog.com/2012/10/the-wars-in-the-
middle-east-and-north-africa-are-not-just-about-oil-theyre-also-about-gas.html
104. integral part: http://www.hydrocarbons-technology.com/projects/arab-gas-
pipeline-agp/
105. additional graphics: http://pipelines.curry.com/
106. from Iran's giant South Pars field through Iraq and Syria:
http://www.aljazeera.com/indepth/opinion/2012/08/201285133440424621.html
107. writes: http://oilprice.com/Energy/Energy-General/Depleted-Global-Oil-and-
Gas-Reserves-have-Led-to-Greater-Interest-in-Syria.html
108. said: http://wlns.com/ap/intelligence-chief-iraq-and-syria-may-not-survive-as-
states-2/
109. decided long ago: http://www.washingtonsblog.com/2014/06/mess-iraq-
design.html
110. noted: http://www.theguardian.com/world/2002/sep/03/worlddispatch.iraq
111. US thinktanks give lessons in foreign policy:
http://www.guardian.co.uk/elsewhere/journalist/story/0,7792,777100,00.html
112. Richard Perle, Paul Wolfowitz, Dick Cheney, John Bolton and others:
http://en.wikipedia.org/wiki/Project_for_the_New_American_Century
113. writes: http://www.counterpunch.org/2014/06/17/is-open-ended-chaos-the-
desired-us-israeli-aim-in-the-middle-east/
114. notes: http://original.antiwar.com/justin/2014/06/17/iraq-will-the-neocons-get-
away-with-it-again/
115. again: http://original.antiwar.com/justin/2003/03/26/iraqi-pandora/
116. again: http://original.antiwar.com/justin/2005/01/31/iraq-election-sistanis-
triumph/
117. real:
http://www.informationclearinghouse.info/pdf/The%20Zionist%20Plan%20for%20t
he%20Middle%20East.pdf

118.years ago: http://original.antiwar.com/justin/2012/01/31/iraq-in-retrospect/
119.dismantled their army:
http://www.slate.com/articles/news_and_politics/war_stories/2007/09/who_disband
ed_the_iraqi_army.html
120.pulverized:
http://www.google.com/search?hl=&q=airstrikes+iraq+2005&sourceid=navclient-
ff&rlz=1B3GGLL_enUS412US413&ie=UTF-8&aq=0&oq=airstrikes+iraq+2005
121.roads: http://www.youtube.com/watch?v=uOrDHKwRXsg&feature=related
122.bridges: http://www.nytimes.com/2007/08/14/world/middleeast/14cnd-
iraq.html
123.electrical plants: http://articles.latimes.com/2005/dec/25/world/fg-power25
124.water facilities: http://waterfortheages.org/2008/04/27/iraq-water-and-politics-
in-a-war-torn-country/
125.museums: http://www.aam-us.org/pubs/mn/MN_JF07_lost-iraq.cfm
126.schools: http://iraqdailytimes.com/education-iraq-iraq-needs-to-5800-schools-
to-meet-the-shortage/
127.dissolved:
http://www.democracynow.org/2010/9/1/iraq_is_a_shattered_country_nir
128.A Clean Break: A New Strategy for Securing the Realm:
http://www.informationclearinghouse.info/article1438.htm
129.declared: http://www.haaretz.com/print-edition/news/sharon-says-u-s-should-
also-disarm-iran-libya-and-syria-1.18707
130.Indeed: http://www.washingtonsblog.com/2011/11/neoconservatives-planned-
regime-change-throughout-the-middle-east-and-northern-africa-20-years-ago.html
131.points out: http://www.globalresearch.ca/the-destruction-and-political-
fragmentation-of-iraq-towards-the-creation-of-a-us-sponsored-islamist-
caliphate/5386998
132.Plans for Redrawing the Middle East: The Project for a "New Middle East":
http://www.globalresearch.ca/plans-for-redrawing-the-middle-east-the-project-for-
a-new-middle-east/3882
133.Mahdi Darius Nazemroaya: http://www.globalresearch.ca/author/mahdi-darius-
nazemroaya
134.wrote: http://www.amazon.com/Zionist-Plan-Middle-Special-
Document/dp/0937694568
135.advocated: http://www.salon.com/2006/08/03/mideast_8/
136.points out: http://www.globalresearch.ca/the-destruction-and-political-
fragmentation-of-iraq-towards-the-creation-of-a-us-sponsored-islamist-
caliphate/5386998
137.key architects: http://www.msnbc.com/msnbc/10-years-later-the-architects-the-
iraq-wa
138.said:: http://www.foxnews.com/transcript/2015/05/24/mike-huckabee-lays-out-
path-to-2016-republican-nomination-amb-john-bolton-talks/
139.Reagan Archives:
http://www.reagan.utexas.edu/archives/photographs/atwork.html
140.admitted: http://www.gwu.edu/%7Ensarchiv/coldwar/interviews/episode-
17/brzezinski1.html
141.organized and supported Bin Laden and the other originators of "Al Qaeda" in
the 1970s: http://www.thenation.com/article/blowback-prequel

142.told: http://www.youtube.com/watch?v=d4lf0RT72iw
143.confirmed: http://www.amazon.com/Shadows-Ultimate-Insiders-Story-Presidents/dp/0684834979/sr=8-1/qid=1163059092/ref=pd_bbs_1/102-8219747-6907339?ie=UTF8&s=books
144.agrees:
http://www.youtube.com/watch?v=Dqn0bm4E9yw?rel=0&controls=0&showinfo=0
145.reported: http://www.msnbc.msn.com/id/3340101/#.UEaKb6BFbKc
146.told: http://www.globalresearch.ca/articles/BRZ110A.html
147.reported:
http://pqasb.pqarchiver.com/washingtonpost/access/110956747.html?FMT=ABS&F
MTS=ABS:FT&date=Mar+23%2C+2002&author=Joe+Stephens+and+David+B.+
Ottaway&pub=The+Washington+Post&edition=&startpage=A.01&desc=From+U.
S.%2C+the+ABC%27s+of+Jihad%3B+Violent+Soviet-
Era+Textbooks+Complicate+Afghan+Education+Efforts
148.notes:
http://www.cfr.org/publication/20364/pakistans_education_system_and_links_to_ex
tremism.html
149.report (PDF): http://www.cfr.org/publication/10353/
150.this: http://www.guardian.co.uk/world/1999/jan/17/yemen.islam
151.Robert Dreyfuss: http://www.robertdreyfuss.com/bio.htm
152.nuclear scientist and peace activist:
http://en.wikipedia.org/wiki/Pervez_Hoodbhoy
153.writes:
http://www.physics.harvard.edu/%7Ewilson/pmpmta/2010_Hoodbhoy.doc
154.says: http://www.youtube.com/watch?v=iw6YHij-aCU
155.well-known: http://www.thenation.com/article/robert-i-friedman
156.wrote: http://books.google.com/books?id=l-
MCAAAAMBAJ&pg=PA43&lpg=PA43&dq=%22According+to+other+sources+f
amiliar+with+the+case,+the+FBI+told+District+Attorney+Robert+M.+Morgenthau
+that+Nosair+was+a+lone+gunman,+not+part+of+a+broader+conspiracy;%22&so
urce=bl&ots=Ri7bd4UFfl&sig=XSFrnaBeJ1cO5a402E6cQRthiPU&hl=en#v=onep
age&q=%22According%20to%20other%20sources%20familiar%20with%20the%2
0case%2C%20the%20FBI%20told%20District%20Attorney%20Robert%20M.%20
Morgenthau%20that%20Nosair%20was%20a%20lone%20gunman%2C%20not%2
0part%20of%20a%20broader%20conspiracy%3B%22&f=false
157.Terror Nation? U.S. Creation?: http://tv.msn.com/tv/episode/cnn-
presents/terror-nation-us-creation/
158.summarized by Congressman Peter Deutsch:
https://www.atsc.army.mil/crc/ISO6A10L/LessonPlan_TheCurrentThreatinAfghani
stan.rtf
159.says: http://www.usnews.com/news/world/articles/2008/07/11/afghan-
warlords-formerly-backed-by-the-cia-now-turn-their-guns-on-us-troops
160.the New York Times:
http://web.archive.org/web/20071212122812/http://pqasb.pqarchiver.com/nytimes/a
ccess/116193080.html?did=116193080&FMT=ABS&FMTS=AI&date=Oct+28,+1
993&author=By+RALPH+BLUMENTHAL&pub=New+York+Times++%281857_
Current+file%29&desc=Tapes+Depict+Proposal+to+Thwart+Bomb+Used+in+Trad
e+Center+Blast

161.CBS News: http://www.youtube.com/watch?v=5F1Y6cGRXEs&eurl

162.supported Bin Laden and other Al Qaeda terrorists in Bosnia:
http://www.amazon.com/Unholy-Terror-Bosnia-Al-Qaida-Global/dp/product-description/0760330034

163.reported: http://www.washingtonsblog.com/2012/11/why-did-cia-director-petraeus-suddenly-resign-and-why-was-the-u-s-ambassador-to-libya-murdered.html

164.largely comprised of Al Qaeda terrorists:
http://www.telegraph.co.uk/news/worldnews/africaandindianocean/libya/8407047/Libyan-rebel-commander-admits-his-fighters-have-al-Qaeda-links.html

165.report: http://www.scribd.com/doc/111001074/West-Point-CTC-s-Al-Qa-ida-s-Foreign-Fighters-in-Iraq

166.reported: http://www.hindustantimes.com/world-news/Americas/Al-Qaeda-present-among-Libyan-rebels/Article1-679511.aspx

167.flown over the Benghazi courthouse:
http://www.washingtonsblog.com/2011/11/did-we-overthrow-gaddafi-just-to-replace-him-with-al-qaeda.html

168.stopped him:
http://www.telegraph.co.uk/news/worldnews/africaandindianocean/libya/8393843/Libya-Benghazi-about-to-fall...-then-came-the-planes.html

169.reported: http://www.dailymail.co.uk/news/article-2610598/Group-US-switched-sides-War-Terror-facilitating-500-MILLION-weapons-deliveries-Libyan-al-Qaeda-militias-leading-Benghazi-attack.html

170.reported: http://www.lrb.co.uk/v36/n08/seymour-m-hersh/the-red-line-and-the-rat-line

171.state: http://www.washingtontimes.com/news/2015/feb/1/hillary-clinton-libya-war-push-armed-benghazi-rebe/print/

172.admitted:
http://www.telegraph.co.uk/news/worldnews/africaandindianocean/libya/8407047/Libyan-rebel-commander-admits-his-fighters-have-al-Qaeda-links.html

173.see this: http://www.washingtonsblog.com/2014/04/real-benghazi-story.html

174.supports terrorists: http://www.washingtonsblog.com/2011/01/biggest-terrorism-scaremongers-are-themselves-promoting-terrorism.html

175.said: http://hammernews.com/odomspeech.htm

176.here: http://hammernews.com/odom.ram

177.reported: http://www.washingtonpost.com/wp-dyn/content/article/2010/08/25/AR2010082506591.html

178.according to a secret CIA analysis released Wednesday by the Web site WikiLeaks:
http://www.wikileaks.com/wiki/CIA_Red_Cell_Memorandum_on_United_States_%22exporting_terrorism%22,_2_Feb_2010

179.notes: http://en.wikipedia.org/wiki/United_States_and_state_terrorism

180.created death squads in Latin America, Iraq and Syria:
http://www.globalresearch.ca/terrorism-with-a-human-face-the-history-of-americas-death-squads/5317564

181."out-terrorize the terrorists": http://www.washingtonsblog.com/2010/09/the-warped-mission-of-the-american-military-out-terrorize-the-terrorists.html

182.notes: http://www.truth-out.org/second-soldier-alleges-former-tillman-commander-ordered-360-rotational-fire-iraq63153

183.defined: http://dictionary.reference.com/browse/terrorism
184.known as: http://en.wikipedia.org/wiki/Mukden_Incident
185.found:
https://books.google.com/books?id=rHainkH7pdEC&pg=PA321&dq=%22Several+
of+the+participators+in+the+plan,+including+Hashimoto,+have+on+various+occas
ions+admitted+their+part+in+the+plot+and+have+stated+that+the+object%22&hl=
en&sa=X&ei=NrOtVLiQGsm6ogT49oCQAg&ved=0CB8Q6AEwAA#v=onepage
&q=%22Several%20of%20the%20participators%20in%20the%20plan%2C%20incl
uding%20Hashimoto%2C%20have%20on%20various%20occasions%20admitted%
20their%20part%20in%20the%20plot%20and%20have%20stated%20that%20the%
20object%22&f=false
186.admitted:
https://books.google.com/books?id=rHainkH7pdEC&pg=PA321&dq=%22Several+
of+the+participators+in+the+plan,+including+Hashimoto,+have+on+various+occas
ions+admitted+their+part+in+the+plot+and+have+stated+that+the+object%22&hl=
en&sa=X&ei=NrOtVLiQGsm6ogT49oCQAg&ved=0CB8Q6AEwAA#v=onepage
&q=%22Several%20of%20the%20participators%20in%20the%20plan%2C%20incl
uding%20Hashimoto%2C%20have%20on%20various%20occasions%20admitted%
20their%20part%20in%20the%20plot%20and%20have%20stated%20that%20the%
20object%22&f=false
187.see this: http://lib.law.virginia.edu/imtfe/person/143
188.admitted: http://en.wikipedia.org/wiki/Gleiwitz_incident
189.admitted:
http://en.wikipedia.org/wiki/Hermann_G%C3%B6ring#Possible_responsibility_for
_the_Reichstag_fire
190.admitted: https://en.wikipedia.org/wiki/Shelling_of_Mainila
191.agreed: https://en.wikipedia.org/wiki/Shelling_of_Mainila
192.admits: http://www.theguardian.com/world/2010/nov/26/russian-parliament-
guilt-katyn-massacre
193.admitted: http://www.theguardian.com/world/2010/nov/26/russian-parliament-
guilt-katyn-massacre
194.admits:
http://www.ynetnews.com/Ext/Comp/ArticleLayout/CdaArticlePrintPreview/1,2506
,L-3065838,00.html#n
195.this: http://www.stanford.edu/group/SHR/5-1/text/beinin.html
196.this: http://www.jewishvirtuallibrary.org/jsource/History/lavon.html
197.admits: http://www.nytimes.com/library/world/mideast/041600iran-cia-
index.html
198.admitted:
http://books.google.com/books?id=SdubdhMwM1YC&pg=PA8&lpg=PA8&dq=the
+riots+were+purportedly+in+response+to+a+september+5+1955+greek+bombing+
attack+on+the+turkish+consulate&source=bl&ots=O7OKEmcJrF&sig=y4vdM7vH
k8Z8g1jH4gXDHTXw400&hl=en&sa=X&ei=z2lKVIuEII3wgwTZ04HICA&ved=
0CCQQ6AEwAQ#v=onepage&q=the%20riots%20were%20purportedly%20in%20
response%20to%20a%20september%205%201955%20greek%20bombing%20attac
k%20on%20the%20turkish%20consulate&f=false
199.admitted: http://www.washingtonsblog.com/2014/07/57-years-ago-u-s-britain-
approved-use-islamic-extremists-topple-syrian-government.html

200.former head of Italian counterintelligence:
http://www.guardian.co.uk/international/story/0,3604,462976,00.html
201.NATO, with the help of the Pentagon and CIA, carried out terror bombings in
Italy and other European countries in the 1950s and blamed the communists, in
order to rally people's support for their governments in Europe in their fight against
communism: http://en.wikipedia.org/wiki/Strategy_of_tension
202."You had to attack civilians, people, women, children, innocent people,
unknown people far removed from any political game. The reason was quite simple.
They were supposed to force these people, the Italian public, to turn to the state to
ask for greater security":
http://web.archive.org/web/20051130003012/http://www.isn.ethz.ch/php/documents
/collection_gladio/synopsis.htm
203.this: http://www.globalresearch.ca/articles/GAN412A.html
204.this BBC special:
https://video.search.yahoo.com/yhs/search;_ylt=AwrTca_5q89UIAwAVlsnnIlQ;_yl
u=X3oDMTB0MzkwOG5yBHNlYwNzYwRjb2xvA2dxMQR2dGlkA1lIUzAwNF8
x?p=bbc+gladio&hspart=mozilla&hsimp=yhs-001
205.France, Belgium, Denmark, Germany, Greece, the Netherlands, Norway,
Portugal, the UK: http://en.wikipedia.org/wiki/Operation_Gladio
206.suggested: http://www.guardian.co.uk/theguardian/2012/aug/17/john-f-
kennedy-fidel-castro
207.discussed: http://www.washingtonsblog.com/2010/02/nine-months-before-
operation-northwoods-government-leaders-suggested-false-flag-terror-in-the-
dominican-republic.html
208.ABC news report: http://abcnews.go.com/US/story?id=92662&page=1
209.the official documents:
http://www.gwu.edu/%7Ensarchiv/news/20010430/northwoods.pdf
210.this interview : http://www.youtube.com/watch?v=IygchZRJVXM
211.promoting:
http://en.wikipedia.org/wiki/Operation_Northwoods#Related_Operation_Mongoose
_proposals
212.suggested:
http://en.wikipedia.org/wiki/Operation_Northwoods#Related_Operation_Mongoose
_proposals
213.admits:
http://www2.gwu.edu/%7Ensarchiv/NSAEBB/NSAEBB132/press20051201.htm
214.lied:
http://web.archive.org/web/20080203204207/http://rawstory.com/news/afp/Report_
reveals_Vietnam_War_hoaxes_f_01082008.html
215.Gulf of Tonkin incident: http://en.wikipedia.org/wiki/Gulf_of_Tonkin_incident
216.admitted: http://www.intelligence.senate.gov/churchcommittee.html
217.top: http://en.wikipedia.org/wiki/Sabri_Yirmibe%C5%9Fo%C4%9Flu
218.admitted:
http://www.hurriyetdailynews.com/default.aspx?pageid=438&n=turkey-burned-
mosque-during-cyprus-war-gen-says-2010-09-24
219.explained: http://www.todayszaman.com/tz-web/news-222544-100-retired-
general-confesses-to-burning-mosque-to-fire-up-public.html
220.admitted: https://en.wikipedia.org/wiki/Celle_Hole

221.see this:
http://translate.google.com/translate?hl=en&sl=de&u=http://www.ndr.de/kultur/ges
chichte/chronologie/cellerloch102.html&prev=/search%3Fq%3Dhttp://www.ndr.de/
kultur/geschichte/cellerloch102.html%26client%3Dfirefox-
a%26hs%3DymV%26rls%3Dorg.mozilla:en-US:official%26channel%3Dsb
222.says: http://www.amazon.com/Way-Deception-Victor-Ostrovsky-
ebook/dp/B002RL9NL2/ref=sr_1_1?s=books&ie=UTF8&qid=1422773938&sr=1-1
223.found: http://www.justice.gov.za/trc/decisions%5C2001/ac21233.htm
224.admit: http://www.encyclopedia.com/doc/1P1-68004301.html
225.this video:
http://www.youtube.com/watch?v=HVJgsb5TuTw&feature=player_embedded
226.elements of the military had been involved in the riots, some of which were
deliberately provoked: http://www.fas.org/irp/world/indonesia/indonesia-1998.htm
227.admit:
http://web.archive.org/web/20060209100406/http://www.telegraph.co.uk/news/mai
n.jhtml?xml=/news/2004/01/13/wrus13.xml
228.this report: http://web.archive.org/web/20080413195430/http://www.sais-
jhu.edu/programs/res/papers/Satter_edited_final.pdf
229.this discussion: http://en.wikipedia.org/wiki/Russian_Apartment_Bombings
230.Washington Post: http://www.highbeam.com/doc/1P2-406202.html
231.admits: http://www.smh.com.au/news/National/Possible-police-role-in-2002-
Bali-attack/2005/10/12/1128796591857.html
232.BBC: http://news.bbc.co.uk/2/hi/europe/3674533.stm
233.New York Times:
http://www.nytimes.com/2004/05/17/international/europe/17mace.html?th=&pagew
anted=all&position=
234.Associated Press: http://www.highbeam.com/doc/1P1-94026683.html
235.admitted:
https://web.archive.org/web/20030207160903/http://www.fair.org/activism/genoa-
update.html
236.violent crackdown: http://www.theguardian.com/world/2010/may/19/g8-
italian-police-sentenced
237.told to blame the Anthrax attacks on Al Qaeda by White House officials:
http://www.nydailynews.com/news/us_world/2008/08/02/2008-08-
02_fbi_was_told_to_blame_anthrax_scare_on_a.html
238.looked like:
http://3.bp.blogspot.com/_MnYI3_FRbbQ/SJLfMP7mkrI/AAAAAAAAA94/irML2
0mNYDA/s400/anthrax.jpg
239.tried to link the anthrax to Iraq:
http://www.nytimes.com/2001/12/22/national/22INQU.html?pagewanted=all
240.falsely blamed Iraq: http://www.washingtonsblog.com/2012/10/5-hours-after-
the-911-attacks-donald-rumsfeld-said-my-interest-is-to-hit-saddam-he-also-said-go-
massive-sweep-it-all-up-things-related-and-not-and-at-2.html
241.memo from the defense secretary:
http://www.washingtonsblog.com/2013/02/newly-released-memos-of-donald-
rumsfeld-prove-knowing-iraq-war.html

242. main justifications: http://www.washingtonsblog.com/2012/10/5-hours-after-the-911-attacks-donald-rumsfeld-said-my-interest-is-to-hit-saddam-he-also-said-go-massive-sweep-it-all-up-things-related-and-not-and-at-2.html
243. admitted: http://www.msnbc.msn.com/id/5223932/ns/us_news-security/t/panel-sees-no-link-between-iraq-al-qaida/#.UIde6fWUxqI
244. said: http://www.cnn.com/2004/ALLPOLITICS/06/18/cheney.iraq.al.qaeda/
245. admit: http://www.washingtonsblog.com/2013/03/top-republican-leaders-say-iraq-war-was-really-for-oil.html
246. say: http://www.washingtonsblog.com/2012/09/government-officials-say-911-was-state-sponsored-terrorism-but-disagree-about-which-nation-was-behind-attacks.html
247. suggested: http://www.aei.org/article/22833
248. reported: http://www.upi.com/Business_News/Security-Industry/2005/06/03/UPI-hears/UPI-64911117829623/
249. admitted: http://mondoweiss.net/2012/05/operation-glass-houses-idf-agent-provocateurs-admit-to-throwing-stones-at-the-idf-in-bilin.html
250. admitted: http://www.youtube.com/watch?v=gAfzUOx53Rg
251. see this: http://www.cbc.ca/news/canada/quebec-police-admit-they-went-undercover-at-montebello-protest-1.656171
252. saw: http://www.guardian.co.uk/politics/2009/may/10/g20-policing-agent-provacateurs
253. admitted: http://www.washingtonsblog.com/2011/01/prominent-former-egyptian-mp-and-presidential-candidate-the-looting-of-the-cairo-museum-was-carried-out-by-government-employees.html
254. see this: http://www.washingtonsblog.com/2011/02/washington-post-confirms-that-egyptian-looters-were-agents-provocateur.html
255. admitted: http://www.bbc.co.uk/news/world-latin-america-14149676
256. admitted: http://www.youtube.com/watch?v=SODTI_C1q_Q
257. admitted: http://www.telegraph.co.uk/finance/newsbysector/energy/oilandgas/10266957/Saudis-offer-Russia-secret-oil-deal-if-it-drops-Syria.html
258. admitted: http://www.washingtonsblog.com/2014/04/nato-member-conducts-false-flag-terror-try-whip-war.html
259. admitted: http://www.washingtonsblog.com/2014/04/nato-member-conducts-false-flag-terror-try-whip-war.html
260. admits: http://www.washingtonsblog.com/2014/03/former-ukranian-security-chief-alleges-new-government-behind-sniper-attacks.html
261. admitted: http://www.washingtonsblog.com/2014/02/nsa-engaged-internet-false-flag-attacks.html
262. see this: http://www.washingtonsblog.com/2014/02/false-flags-honey-traps.html
263. framing people: http://www.washingtonsblog.com/2014/07/spy-agencies-dirty-trick-powers-revealed-snowden.html
264. admitted: http://www.washingtonsblog.com/2014/09/top-u-s-military-official-arab-allies-support-isis.html
265. supporting ISIS: http://www.youtube.com/watch?v=nA39iVSo7XE?start=33
266. agrees: http://www.youtube.com/watch?v=QHLqaSZPe98

267. Vice President Joe Biden:
http://youtube%20http//www.youtube.com/watch?v=w04YE5zRmc8?start=67
268. says: http://www.rawstory.com/rs/2014/08/20/german-minister-accuses-qatar-of-funding-islamic-state-fighters/
269. reports: http://abcnews.go.com/International/hezbollah-al-qaeda-fighters-edging-closer-confrontation/story?id=19144119#.UagnQ5xGR8V
270. headlines: http://www.independent.co.uk/voices/comment/iraq-crisis-how-saudi-arabia-helped-isis-take-over-the-north-of-the-country-9602312.html
271. formerly owned by Newsweek: http://en.wikipedia.org/wiki/The_Daily_Beast
272. notes: http://www.thedailybeast.com/articles/2014/06/14/america-s-allies-are-funding-isis.html
273. told Secretary of State John Kerry:
http://www.independent.co.uk/voices/comment/alqaida-the-second-act-is-saudi-arabia-regretting-its-support-for-terrorism-9198213.html
274. notes: http://www.businessinsider.com/isis-funding-us-allies-2014-6
275. far back as March: http://www.reuters.com/article/2014/03/09/us-iraq-saudi-qatar-idUSBREA2806S20140309
276. December 2013 report:
http://www.brookings.edu/%7E/media/research/files/papers/2013/12/06%20private%20gulf%20financing%20syria%20extremist%20rebels%20sectarian%20conflict%20dickinson/private%20gulf%20financing%20syria%20extremist%20rebels%20sectarian%20conflict%20dickinson.pdf
277. aligned with whatever is left of the Baathist regime once led by Saddam Hussein: http://www.thedailybeast.com/articles/2014/06/14/america-s-allies-are-funding-isis.html
278. directly supporting ISIS: http://www.washingtonsblog.com/2014/09/turkey-israel-directly-supporting-isis-al-qaeda-syria.html
279. Turkey funds the terrorist group: http://www.breitbart.com/Big-Peace/2014/07/30/ISIS-Fighter-Claims-Turkey-Funds-the-Jihadist-Group
280. protecting and cooperating with ISIS and Al Qaeda terrorists:
http://www.hurriyetdailynews.com/chp-lawmakers-accuse-turkish-government-of-protecting-isil-and-al-nusra-militants.aspx?pageID=238&nID=67750&NewsCatID=338
281. medical treatment to ISIS terrorists:
http://www.todayszaman.com/national_nurse-says-shes-tired-of-treating-isil-terrorists_358992.html
282. pointed out: http://time.com/3932515/the-kurds-are-building-a-country-with-every-victory-over-isis/
283. writes: http://time.com/3974399/turkey-kurds-isis/
284. reported: http://www.theguardian.com/world/2015/jul/26/isis-syria-turkey-us?CMP=share_btn_tw
285. Islamic State: http://www.theguardian.com/world/isis
286. Isis official responsible for oil smuggling, named Abu Sayyaf:
http://www.dailymail.co.uk/news/article-3084323/US-special-forces-kill-ISIS-commander.html
287. jihadi groups, such as Ahrar al-Sham:
http://web.stanford.edu/group/mappingmilitants/cgi-bin/groups/view/523

288. long: http://www.washingtonsblog.com/2014/08/allegations-u-s-allies-back-isis-islamic-terrorists.html
289. pointed: http://www.washingtonsblog.com/2014/09/turkey-israel-directly-supporting-isis-al-qaeda-syria.html
290. out: http://www.washingtonsblog.com/2015/02/top-u-s-generals-american-allies-support-isis.html
291. experts: http://www.businessinsider.com/turkey-created-a-monster-and-doesnt-know-how-to-deal-with-it-2015-2
292. Kurds: http://www.newsweek.com/2014/10/31/kurds-accuse-turkish-government-supporting-isis-278776.html
293. Joe Biden: http://www.thegatewaypundit.com/2014/10/turkish-president-erdogan-demands-joe-biden-apologize-for-blaming-turkey-for-rise-of-isis/
294. Israeli air force has bombed: http://www.washingtonsblog.com/2014/12/israel-acts-isis-air-force-repeatedly-bombs-syria.html
295. recently admitted: http://www.washingtonsblog.com/2015/07/israeli-military-admits-to-supporting-syrian-jihadis.html
296. reported: http://www.timesofisrael.com/yaalon-syrian-rebels-keeping-druze-safe-in-exchange-for-israeli-aid/
297. is Al Qaeda, and closely affiliated with ISIS: http://www.washingtonsblog.com/2015/03/us-considering-openly-arming-syrian-al-qaeda-faction-al-nusra.html
298. reported: http://www.timesofisrael.com/syrian-rebel-commander-says-he-collaborated-with-israel/
299. a video: https://www.youtube.com/watch?v=6J1p6HR20_I
300. Safouri was abducted by the al-Qaeda-affiliated Al-Nusra Front: http://www.timesofisrael.com/syrian-al-qaeda-fighters-flee-southward-toward-israel-border/
301. reported: http://www.haaretz.com/news/diplomacy-defense/1.580169
302. noted: http://www.haaretz.com/news/middle-east/.premium-1.576083
303. wrote: http://www.al-monitor.com/pulse/originals/2015/07/israel-syria-war-bashar-al-assad-support-rebels-al-qaeda-is.html
304. emerging alliance: http://www.al-monitor.com/pulse/originals/2015/02/israel-syria-rebels-jihad-sunni-shiite-golan-heights.html
305. choose Assad's enemies: http://www.al-monitor.com/pulse/en/originals/2015/05/moderate-countries-saudi-arabia-israel-jihadists-dictators.html
306. suggests: http://www.thedailybeast.com/articles/2015/08/31/petraeus-use-al-qaeda-fighters-to-beat-isis.html
307. also saying: http://www.washingtonsblog.com/2015/03/mainstream-media-calls-supporting-al-qaeda-isis.html
308. asks: http://www.salon.com/2015/03/18/thomas_friedman_asks_if_us_should_arm_isis_to_fix_problems_created_by_policies_he_supported/
309. says: http://www.infowars.com/former-al-qaeda-commander-isis-works-for-the-cia/
310. the Department of Justice's Inspector General, several senators: http://www.nytimes.com/2005/01/15/national/15translate.html?ex=1153886400&en=13842175814b8e8c&ei=5070

311.coalition of prominent conservative and liberal groups:
http://web.archive.org/web/20071031085021/http://www.libertycoalition.net/state-
secrets-privelage/coalition-letter-to-the-house-committee-on-oversight-and-
government-reform-on-criminal-activities-by-the
312.says: http://www.globalresearch.ca/silencing-a-whistle-blower-gladio-b-and-
the-origins-of-isis-sibel-edmonds/5475126
313.here: http://www.boilingfrogspost.com/2011/11/21/bfp-exclusive-syria-secret-
us-nato-training-support-camp-to-oust-current-syrian-president/
314.here: http://www.boilingfrogspost.com/2011/12/03/us-media-distorters-of-
reality-gravediggers-of-truth/
315.here: http://www.boilingfrogspost.com/2011/12/11/bfp-exclusive-developing-
story-hundreds-of-us-nato-soldiers-arrive-begin-operations-on-the-jordan-syria-
border/
316.here: https://www.youtube.com/watch?v=-v1h1bUfCVc
317.might create a terrorist group like ISIS and an Islamic caliphate:
http://www.washingtonsblog.com/2015/05/newly-declassified-u-s-government-
documents-the-west-supported-the-creation-of-isis.html
318.documents: http://www.judicialwatch.org/wp-content/uploads/2015/05/Pg.-
291-Pgs.-287-293-JW-v-DOD-and-State-14-812-DOD-Release-2015-04-10-final-
version11.pdf
319.years before: http://www.cnn.com/2014/08/08/world/isis-fast-facts/
320.salafists: http://www.washingtonsblog.com/2014/08/closest-u-s-allies-middle-
east-hotbeds-islamic-fundamentalism.html
321.aren't any moderate rebels: http://www.washingtonsblog.com/2014/09/war-
3.html
322.this: https://www.google.com/search?q=no+moderate+rebels+syria&ie=utf-
8&oe=utf-8&aq=t&rls=org.mozilla:en-US:official&client=firefox-a&channel=sb
323.this:
http://www.washingtonpost.com/blogs/worldviews/wp/2014/10/06/behind-bidens-
gaffe-some-legitimate-concerns-about-americas-middle-east-allies/
324.this: http://news.firedoglake.com/2014/08/11/obama-admits-arming-moderate-
syrian-rebels-has-always-been-a-fantasy/
325.confirm: https://medium.com/insurge-intelligence/secret-pentagon-report-
reveals-west-saw-isis-as-strategic-asset-b99ad7a29092
326.served as: https://en.wikipedia.org/wiki/Michael_T._Flynn
327.confirmed:
http://www.youtube.com/watch?v=SG3j8OYKgn4?start=675&end=769
328.NBC News: http://www.nbcnews.com/storyline/middle-east-unrest/u-s-
launches-airstrikes-aid-american-trained-syrian-rebels-n401906
329.Wall Street Journal: http://www.wsj.com/articles/u-s-to-give-some-syria-rebels-
ability-to-call-airstrikes-1424208053?mod=djemalertNEWS
330.CNN: http://www.cnn.com/2015/08/02/middleeast/syrian-rebels-u-s-air-cover/
331.U.S. trained Islamic jihadis – who would later join ISIS :
http://www.wnd.com/2014/06/officials-u-s-trained-isis-at-secret-base-in-jordan/
332.confirmed: http://www.reuters.com/article/2013/03/10/us-syria-crisis-rebels-
usa-idUSBRE9290FI20130310

333.more in common with Mao's Red Guards or the Khmer Rouge than it does with the Muslim empires of antiquity: https://firstlook.org/theintercept/2014/09/26/isis-islamic/
334.reports: http://www.huffingtonpost.co.uk/mehdi-hasan/jihadist-radicalisation-islam-for-dummies_b_5697160.html?utm_hp_ref=tw
335.Here's the Guardian report:
http://www.theguardian.com/uk/2008/aug/20/uksecurity.terrorism1
336.foreign occupation – and not religion:
http://www.washingtonsblog.com/2013/10/u-s-war-on-terror-has-increased-terrorism.html
337.top Bin Laden hunter agreed: http://www.washingtonsblog.com/2014/07/head-cia-unit-tasked-killing-bin-laden.html
338.Muslim leaders worldwide condemn ISIS:
http://www.washingtonsblog.com/2014/08/muslims-condemn-isis.html
339.this:
http://web.archive.org/web/20011010224657/http://www.bostonherald.com/attack/investigation/ausprob10102001.htm
340.this: http://web.archive.org/web/20010916150533/http://www.sun-sentinel.com/news/local/southflorida/sfl-warriors916.story
341.this: http://www.newsweek.com/2001/10/14/cracking-the-terror-code.html
342.this:
http://web.archive.org/web/20011023132702/http://interactive.wsj.com/articles/SB1003180286455952120.htm
343.this:
http://web.archive.org/web/20090213114442/http://articles.latimes.com/2002/sep/01/nation/na-plot
344.this:
http://www.historycommons.org/context.jsp?item=a091101beforepinkpony#a091101beforepinkpony
345.this: http://www.firstcoastnews.com/news/local/story.aspx?storyid=23296
346.this: http://www.youtube.com/embed/_qC0rEG_f3Y

Born of the USA:
The Real Origins of ISIL

By Wayne Madsen

The comments of two U.S. generals, one active duty and the other retired, exposed for the entire world the covert U.S. backing enjoyed by the Islamic State of Iraq and the Levant (ISIL) in its rise to power in Syria and Iraq. The retired director of the Defense Intelligence Agency, Lieutenant General Michael Flynn, revealed that U.S. support for the most radical Islamist guerrillas in Syria led to the creation of the Islamic State in that country. Provided with arms via a Central Intelligence Agency (CIA)-initiated covert supply chain from post-Muammar Qaddafi Libya, itself decimated by a U.S. - and NATO-created civil war, ISIL was successful in seizing territory from the Syrian government of President Bashar al-Assad. ISIL then turned its attention to Iraq and seized a large swath of territory in Iraq's western and northern regions. The net result of this U.S. backing for the Islamic State was the creation of a brutal Islamic Caliphate stretching from the outskirts of Baghdad and Damascus to eastern Libya, northern Nigeria, and pockets in Egypt's Sinai Peninsula.

The ISIL insurgents, many of them foreign mercenaries who are considered more dangerous than Al Qaeda by many Pentagon and U.S. intelligence specialists, have disturbing links to intelligence services of the United States, Israel, France, and Britain.

The deeper one digs into the operations surrounding the ISIL, or, as it is variably called, "Islamic State of Iraq and al-Sham" (ISIS), "Al Dawlah" (the State), or "Da'ish" (an acronym of *"al-Dawla al-Islamiya fi Iraq wa al-Sham"*), the more the Islamist insurgent group's links to Western and Israeli intelligence are revealed. ISIL is an outgrowth of the Organization of Jihad's Base in the Country of the Two Rivers or Al Qaeda in Iraq (AQI), which was once led by Abu Musab al-Zarqawi. As with the current leader of ISIL, Abu Bakr al-Baghdadi, questions also surrounded the background of Zarqawi.

Zarqawi's real name was Ahmed Fadeel Nazal al-Khalayleh. He was born in the Jordanian town of Zarqa. Abu Musab al-Zarqawi was an alias as much as Abu Bakr al-Baghdadi was an alias for the alleged leader of ISIL. Al Baghdadi, a native of Samarra, Iraq, was actually Ibrahim ibn Awwad ibn Ibrahim ibn Ali ibn Muhammad al-Badri al-Samarrai. Before he joined the mujaheddin war against the Soviets in Afghanistan, Zarqawi was a video store clerk who was known as a

drunk and drug abuser, hardly material for the fundamentalist
Islamists bankrolled by Saudi Arabia and the Gulf emirates.

After the American invasion of Iraq, Zarqawi proclaimed himself
the "Emir of Al Qaeda in the Country of the Two Rivers" and he
quickly became public enemy number one for U.S. occupation forces.
Zarqawi was recruited in Jordan by "The Base" or "Al Qaeda" to serve
in the ranks of Arab legions fighting the Soviets in Afghanistan. As
the late British Foreign Secretary pointed out, "The Base" or "Al
Qaeda" was a CIA database containing the names of various CIA
recruiters, financiers, exporters, and other personnel required to
maintain the flow of mercenaries, weapons, and money to
Afghanistan and Pakistan to sustain the campaign against the Soviets
in Afghanistan.[1]

Al Qaeda leader Osama bin Laden was also allegedly known to the
CIA by his agency cover name "Tim Osman" and by his Arab Afghani
volunteers as the "Hero of Jaji." Jaji was the location of an Afghan
battlefield where Bin Laden was victorious against the Soviets.
Reports of Bin Laden's past connections to the CIA, including an
alleged arms procurement meeting he held with CIA agents in
Sherman Oaks, California in 1986, have been relegated to relatively
obscure publications and websites in an obvious campaign by the CIA
to downplay its one-time association with the jihadist insurgent
leader.[2] In fact, it is known that Bin Laden ran the *Maktab al-
Khidamar* - the MAK - for the CIA and Saudis. MAK ensured the flow
of fighters, money, and weapons to the Afghan insurgency on behalf
of the CIA's Al Qaeda operation.

After the Soviets withdrew from Afghanistan, Zarqawi, who
befriended Bin Laden, returned to Jordan but was jailed by the
authorities for setting up *Jund al-Sham*, a "caliphate" liberation
movement with the goal of establishing an Islamist state in Syria,
Lebanon, Jordan, Palestine, Cyprus, and southern Turkey. It is no
coincidence that *Jund al-Sham* had similar goals to those of the later-
proclaimed Islamic State. It also turned out that *Jund al-Sham* was
thoroughly infiltrated by Jordanian intelligence,[3] which informed the
CIA about all the group's members.

---

[1] Robin Cook, "The struggle against terrorism cannot be won by military means,"
The Guardian, July 8, 2005.
[2] Mike Blair, "Public Enemy No. 1 was guest of the Central Intelligence Agency,"
American Free Press, January 7/14, 2002.
[3] Harmony Project, Combating Terrorism Center at West Point, *Al Qaeda's
(Mis)Adventures in the Horn of Africa*, Darby, PA: Diane Publishing, 2009. p. 122.

Zarqawi was released by Jordan in 2001. He traveled to Afghanistan to battle against the U.S. occupation forces there and he eventually found his way into Iraq where he organized jihadists for the forthcoming U.S. invasion. CIA "evidence" that Zarqawi was in Iraq was used to justify the 2003 U.S. invasion of the country. Jordanian intelligence and the CIA also had evidence that Zarqawi was involved in the 2005 bombings in Amman of the Radisson SAS Hotel, the Grand Hyatt, and the Days Inn. The attacks were used by Jordan and the U.S. to beef up America's military presence in the Hashemite Kingdom.

One time CIA deputy director Michael Morell wrote that Zarqawi's and AQI's rise to power in Iraq were a direct result of two schemes by the Bush administration neocons in the wake of the U.S. occupation of Iraq. One was the edict by the U.S. Coalition Provisional Authority to "remove anyone who had been a member of Saddam's Baath Party from a position inside the Iraqi government." The second was "to disband any organization with close ties to the Baath Party," which "resulted in the collapse of the Iraqi military and security services." Morell wrote that the resulting vacuum was filled by, among others, AQI.[4] It cannot be stressed enough that the neocons in charge of Iraq knew that the country would fall into the hands of jihadists financed by the Saudis and armed and trained by Al Qaeda.

Beginning in 2003, Zarqawi was accused of carrying out a number of terrorist attacks against Western interests inside Iraq, as well as in Casablanca, Madrid, and Istanbul. Zarqawi's base of operations in Iraq was in the northern Kurdistan region, in the area later claimed by ISIL and Baghdadi. In May 2004, AQI released a video in which American Nick Berg was claimed by the CIA to have been beheaded by a masked Zarqawi. The video allegedly posted by AQI was "found" on the Internet by the Washington, DC-based Search for International Terrorist Entities Institute or "SITE," run by Rita Katz, an individual with close ties to Israel's Mossad. The Berg beheading was the only video said to have been made by Zarqawi. Zarqawi's other media releases in which he issued threats against the West were audio recordings. Although the CIA stated that it confirmed Zarqawi's voice on the Berg beheading video, there were no independent verifications of Zarqawi's voice being on either the beheading videotape or the various audio recordings.

Zarqawi's exploits in Iraq were hyped further after he was said to have personally beheaded in September 2004 American contractor

---

[4] Michael Morell, *The Great War of Our Time*, New York: Twelve, 2015, pp. 305-6.

Owen Eugene Armstrong, an employee of Gulf Supplies Commercial Services of the United Arab Emirates, and supposedly ordered the beheading of British engineer Ken Bigley in October 2004. Zarqawi was also said to have ordered the 2002 assassination of U.S. diplomat Lawrence Foley in Jordan and the bombing in August 2003 of the Canal Hotel in Baghdad, the headquarters of the United Nations, an attack that killed United Nations Secretary General's special envoy Sergio Vieira de Mello and 21 other people. Zarqawi became the name the U.S. associated with almost every Sunni terrorist attack in Iraq, including the 2006 bombing of the Shi'a al-Askari Mosque in Samarra, Shi'a shrines in Karbala and Najaf, and thousands of killings of Iraqi civilians. A document later found in one of Zarqawi's Iraq safe houses revealed plans for him to goad the U.S. into attacking Iran. Such a plan would have fit in nicely with U.S. Vice President Dick Cheney's and Israel's long range goals for the region.

In his February 5, 2003, address to the UN Security Council, Secretary of State Colin Powell, who lied about Iraq possessing biological weapons of mass destruction and mobile bio-warfare laboratories, also stated that Saddam Hussein was linked to Zarqawi. Iraq's intelligence service later stated that it could not even locate Zarqawi in Iraq. Unquestionably, Zarqawi was as much a threat to Saddam as he was to the U.S. or Jordan. Had Saddam captured the jihadist leader, he would have likely been tortured for information and then executed on the spot and on Saddam's personal orders.

In the 2006 Senate Report on Prewar Intelligence, the Senate Intelligence Committee concluded: "Postwar information indicates that Saddam Hussein attempted, unsuccessfully, to locate and capture al-Zarqawi and that the regime did not have a relationship with, harbor, or turn a blind eye toward Zarqawi."[5] It turned out that the "intelligence" linking Zarqawi to Saddam had emanated from the Pentagon's notorious Mossad mole, Undersecretary of Defense for Policy and Plans Douglas Feith, who leaked the information in a classified memorandum to Stephen Hayes, the columnist for the neo-conservative *Weekly Standard*.

Zarqawi: The man and the myth

Some U.S. intelligence sources claimed that Zarqawi was a "myth" invented by the neocons to justify continued U.S. military operations in Iraq. Iraqi Sunni and Shi'a leaders rarely agree, however. A Sunni insurgent leader told *The Daily Telegraph* that he believed that

---

[5] Mark Mazzetti, "C.I.A. Said to Find No Hussein Link to Terror Chief," *The New York Times*, September 9, 2006.

Zarqawi was an American or Israeli agent[6] and Iraqi Shi'a leader
Muqtada al Sadr claimed that Zarqawi was a fake *takfir* (a Muslim
who declares that other Muslims, such as the Shia's, are heretics) and
was in the employment of the United States. Shi'a imam Sheikh
Jawad Al-Khalessi repeated the accusation that Zarqawi was a myth
in 2005. According to *The Washington Post*, General Mark Kimmitt,
the U.S. Central Command's chief public affairs officer in Iraq stated
in a 2004 internal CENTCOM briefing that "The Zarqawi PSYOP
program is the most successful information campaign to date."[7]

The Afghan Northern Alliance claimed that Zarqawi was killed in a
2002 missile attack in Afghanistan. There were a number of reports
of Zarqawi having been killed by either U.S. missiles or bombs in
2003. Some reports claimed that Zarqawi had lost a leg in Afghan
combat operations. Other reports said he had both of his legs. The
"Zarqawi" in the Berg beheading video had both legs, and an autopsy
X-ray of the person said to have been Zarqawi and who was
reportedly killed in a 2006 U.S. air strike showed a fracture to the
lower right leg, said to have been lost in Afghanistan.

Zarqawi was captured in Iraq by coalition forces in 2004 but
released. The explanation given at the time was that the Iraqis and
Americans failed to recognize America's public enemy number one in
Iraq. Zarqawi's eventual successor as the head of AQI, al-Baghdadi,
was also captured by U.S. forces in Iraq in 2004 and held at Camp
Bucca from February to December 2004 before being released. Al-
Baghdadi took over the AQI operation in May 2010 after his
predecessor Abu Omar al-Qurashi al-Baghdadi, actual name Hamid
Dawud Mohamed Khalil al Zawi, was killed in a U.S.-Iraqi rocket
attack. In 2007, Bin Laden intermediary Khaled al-Mashhadani, also
known as Abu Shahid, claimed Abu Omar al-Baghdadi, the
predecessor to the current ISIL chief, was a fictional character
designed by Al Qaeda in Iraq to give an Iraqi face to a foreign-led
insurgency. Mashhadani said audio statements attributed to Abu
Omar were being read by an Iraqi actor.[8] Suspiciously, the Abu Omar
recordings were all released by the SITE Institute.

U.S. forces claimed they killed Zarqawi near Baqubah, Iraq in a
June 7, 2006 targeted killing by two precision-guided bombs.

---

[6] Obituary, Abu Musab al-Zarqawi, *The Daily Telegraph*, June 9, 2006.

[7] Thomas Ricks, "Military Plays Up Role of Zarqawi," *The Washington Post*, April
9, 2006.

[8] Dean Yates, Reuters, "Senior Qaeda figure in Iraq a myth: U.S. military," July 18,
2007.

Enter Al-Baghdadi II

While Zarqawi was hyped as one of America's most dangerous enemies, the man who eventually succeeded him as the head of ISIL in Syria, Abu Bakr al-Baghdadi, became one of America's trusted allies. Al-Baghdadi, along with the leaders of the Al Nusra Front, initially placed their forces under the umbrella of the Free Syrian Army. In May 2013, U.S. Senator John McCain, a chief water carrier for the neocon interventionists and Israeli interests, covertly met with Syrian rebel leaders after crossing into rebel-held Syrian territory from Turkey. McCain was accompanied by General Salem Idris, the head of the Free Syrian Army's Supreme Military Council, as he met with the commanders of a number of Syrian rebel units.

One of these rebel commanders was none other than Abu Bakr al-Baghdadi, the current head of ISIL. McCain's office has denied that Al-Baghdadi was present at the meetings, but photographic evidence of the ISIL chief's meeting with McCain and the U.S.-supported Free Syrian Army officials is overwhelming.

The Commander of the U.S. Special Operations Command, General Lloyd Austin, testified before the Senate Armed Services Committee in September 2015 that, to date, the United States had trained a

grand total of "four or five" moderate Syrian fighters in the alleged U.S. war against ISIL.[9] Hundreds of millions of dollars had been spent on the Pentagon's "train and equip" program for the alleged Syrian "moderates," however, the money seemed to have gone elsewhere. Austin's testimony revealed, perhaps unwittingly, that American weapons and training had found their way into the hands of ISIL and allied groups like Al Nusra Front and Khorasan Group.

America's response to ISIL's threat to turn Iraq, Syria, Lebanon, Jordan, and other countries into an Islamic Caliphate were as perplexing as American indifference over proclaimed caliphates by initially U.S.-supported Islamist radicals in Libya and by Boko Haram in Nigeria and Ansar Dine in Mali. The lackadaisical attitude by the CIA and the White House over these groups, which kidnapped, raped, tortured, burned, bombed, and beheaded their way into international headlines, was exactly what would be expected from a scenario in which radical Islamist groups were created by the CIA, Mossad, and MI-6 to create permanent conflict situations between the West and Islam, and between Muslims themselves.

"Al-Baghdadi II" – a contrivance of Mossad and Western intelligence agencies

There is a wealth of material to strongly suggest that America's "public enemy number one" during its occupation of Iraq, Abu Musab al-Zarqawi and the "two al-Baghdadis" – Omar and Abu Bakr – who followed him, were psychological warfare creations of the CIA, Mossad, and the British MI-6 Secret Intelligence Service.

Abu Bakr al-Baghdadi, or "Al Baghdadi II," released audio statements claiming that he is the new caliph of the Islamic State, that he would march on Rome to conquer the Mediterranean region, including all of Spain and Italy for his caliphate, and that he will kill Russian President Vladimir Putin and Pope Francis I. There are elements in Wall Street and in the power centers of Washington, London, and Jerusalem that would not have minded at all if Putin and the Pope were "eliminated," and if it were done by ISIL, so much the better for Western globalization plans.

But was "al-Baghdadi II" real or as much a fake as Zarqawi?

Nabil Na'eem, a former top Al Qaeda commander and founder of the Islamic Democratic Jihad Party in Lebanon, told Beirut's Al-Maydeen television network that ISIL is a creation of the CIA and

---

[9] Luis Martinez, "General Austin: Only '4 or 5' US-Trained Syrian Rebels Fighting ISIS," ABC News, September 16, 2015.

Mossad. Na'eem also stated that the intent of ISIL is to implement Israeli Prime Minister Binyamin Netanyahu's "Clean Break" policy that dates from the 1990s.[10] Al-Baghdadi II is reported to have undergone Mossad military and Islamist theology training in Israel for a year. Na'eem also said that the commander of the Al-Nusra Front, Mohammed al-Jawlani, who swore allegiance to ISIL, is a CIA operative.[11]

A videotaped speech by Al Baghdadi at the Great Mosque of al-Nuri in Mosul, in which he claimed to be the caliph of all Muslims, was deemed a fake by an Iraqi government official.

There is every indication that ISIL had significant links to Israel. Although there are claims to the contrary, ISIL absorbed most of the ranks of the Al Qaeda-affiliated Jabhat al-Nusra (Al Nusra Front) Islamist insurgent group in Syria. Al Nusra Front coordinated its seizure of Syrian army positions along the Golan Heights border with the Israeli Defense Force (IDF). Rather than hit back at Al Nusra positions on the Syrian side of the Golan frontier, the Israelis attacked Syrian army positions, giving a boost to the Syrian campaigns of Al Nusra in particular and ISIL in general. There were reports that the Israeli military was given the coordinates of Syrian army and Hezbollah forces, as well as "Committees for the Defense of the Homeland" militia forces of Alawites, Shi'as, Christians, and Druze, by Al-Nusra/ISIL to launch missile and drone attacks from the Israeli side of the border.

Israel was so sanguine about ISIL, the Israeli daily *Ha'aretz* reported, that Israeli authorities routinely permitted Israeli tourists, armed only with cameras and binoculars, to visit the Golan Heights and peer out over the valley of Quneitra to witness Al-Nusra/ISIL jihadists fighting the Syrian army. Israel even supplied large telescopic viewers for Israelis to spy on the fighting in the valley.[12] Israelis, some who brought their lunch, coffee, and lawn chairs, spent the entire day watching Arabs killing other Arabs. The Israeli complacency about the jihadists suggested a deal had been worked out between the Israeli government and the Syrian jihadists not to

---

[10] The Clean Break was complementary to the 1982 "Yinon Plan," crafted by Likud Party loyalist and journalist Oded Yinon, which called for the destruction of the modern Arab nation-states and their replacement with warring caliphates and warlords.

[11] Wayne Madsen, "The Looming American Quagmire in Iraq and Syria," Strategic Culture Foundation, September 19, 2014.

[12] Judy Maltz, "On Golan, Israelis Grab a Front-row Seat to the War in Syria, *Ha'aretz*, September 7, 2014.

bring the conflict across the Golan frontier into Israel. Or, the Syrian jihadists were under some type of operational control by Mossad and the IDF, and were under strict orders to not attack Israeli targets under any circumstance.

After Al-Nusra/ISIL rebels seized control of United Nations peacekeeping facilities in the Golan, Philippines Army chief General Gregorio Catapang stated that the UN's French Under-Secretary-General for Peacekeeping Operations, Herve Ladsous, ordered 81 Philippines troops to hand their weapons over the jihadists. Although the Philippines troops refused Ladsous's order and were subsequently permitted to "escape" into Israel, there was no information on the fate of 45 Fijian peacekeepers captured by Al-Nusra/ISIL. Nor was Ladsous forthcoming on what happened to the Fijians' weapons.

Catapang also stated that the UNDOF (United Nations Disengagement and Observation Force) Commander, General Iqbal Singh Singha of India, wanted the Philippines peacekeepers to hand over their weapons to the jihadists because of a demand by the rebels that they would harm their Fijian captives if they did not surrender their weapons. Catapanga's Fijian counterpart, Fiji Army Chief Brigadier General Mosese Tikoitoga, stated that it was Singha who ordered the 45 Fijian peacekeepers, most if not all of them being Christians, to surrender to Al Nusra/ISIL, along with handing over of their weapons to the terrorists. Al-Nusra/ISIL intended to try the Fijians under Islamic sharia law for "war crimes."[13] Without the UNDOF force present in the Golan, Israel was able to violate the UN cease fire agreement at will and move weapons and personnel across the Syrian frontier in support of Al-Nusra/ISIL.

It was later reported that Singha and Ladsous also ordered Irish peacekeeping troops who served at the Breiqa UN encampment with the Philippines troops to also surrender to Al-Nusra/ISIL, enriching the Islamist terrorists with even more captured weapons. The Irish troops were permitted to "escape" into Israel with the assistance of the IDF.

Ultimately, the decision to order the Philippines and Fijian troops to surrender to Al-Nusra/ISIL rested on Under-Secretary-General for Political Affairs Jeffrey Feltman, a former U.S. ambassador to Lebanon and Undersecretary of State for Near Eastern Affairs who was a rock solid member of the neocon and Israel agent-of-influence

---

[13] ABS-CBN News, "UN backs Golan commander, denies PH's claims," September 4, 2014.

infrastructure and who wormed his way from the State Department into the UN. Feltman was champion of arming Syrian rebels, including the Islamists, against the Assad government and Hezbollah volunteers from Lebanon. Feltman also served in the U.S. embassy in Tel Aviv in the 1990s during the time when U.S. ambassador Martin Indyk, a key agent-of-influence for Israel, lost his security clearance after a compromise of classified U.S. information to the Israeli government. Secretary of State Madeleine Albright, yet another water carrier for Israel, quickly restored Indyk's security clearance after a watered-down official "investigation." A U.S. embassy Tel Aviv source revealed that among the information compromised were the codes used for secure telephone units to discuss classified information between the embassy and the U.S. government in Washington.

The American grand master for Israel's expansionist policies, former U.S. Secretary of State Henry Kissinger, stated that Iran was a bigger threat than ISIL.[14] Prospective Democratic presidential candidate Hillary Clinton had earlier lavished praise on Kissinger in a review of his new book, *World Order*. Kissinger's comments came after reports that the U.S. military was coordinating its attacks on ISIL in northern Iraq with Iranian Revolutionary Guard forces that were aiding Kurdish Peshmerga forces in Iraqi Kurdistan, and a day after Iran's Supreme Ayatollah, Ali Hosseini *Khamenei*, ordered Iran's forces to cooperate with the United States in attacking ISIL. Kissinger, in his usual role as an agent-of-influence for Israel, sloughed off ISIL as a "group of adventurers" who would have to conquer more territory to become as threatening as Iran. Kissinger's giving a pass to ISIL appeared coordinated with Israel's tacit support for the group. Ever since Netanyahu commissioned the "Clean Break" policy in the early 1990s, it was the wish of the Zionist parties in Israel to not only kill off the Palestinian peace process and absorb the West Bank, Gaza, and the Golan Heights into Israel, but also to create ethnic and religious divisions in various Arab countries, with a goal of creating Israeli-managed statelets. That policy came to full fruition in Syria, Iraq, Libya, and Yemen.

The beheading videos

Just as Zarqawi was said to have beheaded British engineer Bigley in 2004, Al-Baghdadi II ordered the beheading of British contractor David Cawthorne Haines. Bigley's videotaped beheading by AQI came after the videotaped beheadings of Americans Berg and

---

[14] "Kissinger: Iran Is a Bigger Threat Than Islamic State," *Ha'aretz*, September 7, 2014.

Armstrong. Ten years later, ISIL beheaded the Briton Haines after the videotaped beheadings of U.S. journalist James Foley and dual-nationality U.S.-Israeli journalist Steven Sotloff.

It was a London-accented ISIL jihadist who allegedly beheaded Foley and Sotloff. Known as "Jihad John" and said to be London rapper Abdel-Majed Abdel Bary, a British-Egyptian, the alleged beheader reportedly received his inspiration from British Muslim cleric Anjem Choudary, who was permitted to use London to issue pro-ISIL statements. The beheading of the Briton and Americans came as British Prime Minister David Cameron issued an elevated alert for ISIL-led terrorism in the United Kingdom. It appeared that Cameron's gambit was to scare Scottish independence referendum voters into opting for continued "protection" from Merry Old England.

President Obama was always reluctant to order a massive U.S. military attack on ISIL. Was that because he knew that his Saudiphile CIA chief, John O. Brennan, authorized the training of ISIL guerrillas at a secret base near the town of Safawi in Jordan's northern desert region and at another installation near the American airbase at Incirlik in Turkey? Was the initial reluctance of Britain and France to engage ISIL the result of their military instructors helping the CIA train ISIL insurgents at Safawi and Incirlik?

There were also questions about the "journalistic" roles of Foley and Sotloff in covering the wars in Syria, Libya, and Iraq. The two both had a very questionable relationship with a combination freelance videographer and mercenary from Baltimore named Matthew VanDyke.

VanDyke fought with Islamist guerrillas against Muammar Qaddafi's forces during the Libyan civil war and was detained by the Qaddafi government, along with Foley, for entering Libya illegally and being found embedded with rebel forces. Sotloff also covered Libya from the vantage point of the Islamist insurgent forces, some of whom later took control of Tripoli. VanDyke, Foley, and Sotloff also entered Syria illegally and reported only from the ranks of the Islamist guerrilla side. E-mail was released between journalists for *The New York Times, The Wall Street Journal, The Washington Post,* and other publications on one hand and the CIA on the other showing collusion between the reporters and the CIA in writing stories. Questions were also raised about Foley's relationship with the seemingly under-capitalized but worldwide-present *GlobalPost.com* of Boston and why Sotloff, who wrote for a publication owned by the neo-conservative *Jerusalem Post*, was embedded with Islamist *takfiris*,[15] and even had his Twitter photograph taken manning a jihadist truck-mounted machine gun in Syria. The *Journalist Creed* deters such practices, whether they were alleged journalist VanDyke fighting with guerrillas in Libya, or Sotloff manning an insurgent machine gun in Syria, or Foley only embedding with Islamist guerrillas in Syria or Libya.

After writing an article about the CIA's possible use of journalists in covert operations abroad, an overturning of a longtime ban on such practices, this writer was immediately attacked by the Israeli-friendly on-line media. Evidently, a very sensitive nerve was hit.

McCain's consorting with terrorists exposed

Senator McCain's links to ISIL pointed to the close links between the group and a network in Washington that not only includes McCain, the chairman of the Senate Armed Services Committee, but also to Brennan's CIA.

McCain's Middle East adviser Elizabeth O'Bagy, who falsely claimed to have had a PhD from Georgetown University, accompanied McCain on an unofficial trip to Syria in 2013 where the two met and were photographed with Abu Bakr al-Baghdadi and Mohammed Nour of the Northern Storm Brigade of the ISIL-linked Al Nusra Front. Standing next to Salim Idriss, the former head of the Supreme Military Council of the "Free Syrian Army" who lived in exile in Doha, Qatar, was O'Bagy.

While McCain was meeting with Nour, the Northern Storm Brigade had already kidnapped Shi'a pilgrims in Syria, as well as a Lebanese journalist. Had any other Americans met with documented terrorists such as Nour and al-Baghdadi, unlike McCain and O'Bagy, they would have been arrested and charged with aiding and abetting a terrorist group. Several Americans were serving long prison terms for doing much less than McCain and O'Bagy had done in Syria and were entrapped in FBI sting operations merely because they were Muslims.

At the time O'Bagy accompanied McCain to Syria to meet in Bab Salama with the chief of ISIL and other terrorist leaders, including 20 Syrian rebel brigade commanders representing Al Nusra and the

---

[15] The term derives from the root "Kaffir" or infidel, unbeliever. A *takfiri* is one who calls everyone else an apostate. Like the old story of the two bums in the slums. One said, "The whole world is crazy, except us." The other replied, "Yep – and I'm not too sure about you."

Seriously, *takfiri* is a more accurate term than "jihadist," because *Jihad* does not mean a holy war or a crusade, it is a general term for any kind of struggle.

nascent ISIL, O'Bagy worked for Kimberly Kagan, the wife of arch-neocon Zionist Frederick Kagan of the right-wing American Enterprise Institute, and sister-in-law of Robert Kagan, a resident neocon scholar at the Brookings Institution, and his wife, Victoria Nuland, the neo-conservative Assistant Secretary for European and Eurasian Affairs at the State Department. Nuland was primarily responsible for funding and coordinating the coup in Ukraine that resulted in a bloody civil war between Russian-speaking eastern Ukraine and the Nazi- and Zionist-dominated central government in Kiev.

Working under Kimberly Kagan, O'Bagy was the Syria analyst in the Institute for the Study of War (ISW), another neocon operation in Washington that wielded undue influence over U.S. foreign policy in the Middle East and elsewhere. After it was disclosed that she committed resumé fraud by falsely claiming to have a PhD from Georgetown, O'Bagy was officially "fired" by ISW but continued on as the Political Director of the Syrian Emergency Task Force (SETF) NGO, a nonprofit that sought donations from other NGOs, including the neoconservative Freedom House and the Foundation for the Defense of Democracies. SETF admitted to having "sub-contracts with the U.S. and British governments to provide aid to the Syrian opposition." O'Bagy also served officially as a legislative assistant to McCain. The SETF was an extreme anti-Bashar al-Assad organization that used Pentagon-grade psychological warfare tactics to demonize the Assad government and falsely blame him for atrocities carried out by Syrian rebels, including sarin and chlorine gas attacks in Syria.

O'Bagy's operations security (OPSEC) left something to be desired as she voraciously sent out Twitter messages during her clandestine visit to Syria with McCain in 2013. After the visit was publicized, O'Bagy deleted her Twitter messages.

O'Bagy was most infamous for writing an August 30, 2013 Op-Ed in *The Wall Street Journal* that was cited by both McCain and Secretary of State John Kerry. The article, titled "On the Front Lines of Syria's Civil War," was cited by McCain during a Senate hearing as "an important op-ed by *Dr.* Elizabeth O'Bagy." Kerry also cited the article in testimony before the House Foreign Affairs Committee, calling it a "very interesting article." [16]

In the article, O'Bagy, who claimed to have made a number of trips to Syria to liaise with Syrian rebels, falsely stated that Syrian

[16] Elizabeth O'Bagy, "On the Front Lines of Syria's Civil War," *The Wall Street Journal*, August 30, 2013.

"moderates" were leading the fight against the Syrian government in Damascus. The Op-Ed called for the United States to provide "sophisticated weaponry" to the rebels and enter the civil war militarily. Obama refused to follow this advice, a decision that earned him the scorn of McCain and other neocons. McCain continued to suggest that the Syrian "moderate" rebels had a chance to seize control of Syria.

In her "tweets," O'Bagy took responsibility for everything from McCain's attire in Syria to the individuals with whom he met. It was later learned that these individuals not only included al-Baghdadi and Nour, but other terrorist commanders. O'Bagy was also at pains to distance her Syrian rebel friends from Abu Sakkar, aka Khalid bin Hamad, the rebel commander who was filmed eating the heart of a Syrian soldier. O'Bagy denied that Abu Sakkar was a member of the Free Syrian Army's Homs-based Farooq Brigades, but independent news reports stated that he was indeed a commander of the brigades. O'Bagy also misidentified bin Hamad as a non-threatening Farouq Mustaqila, a familiar tactic of the neocons and no surprise from an individual who lied about having a PhD.

ISIL and the Saudis, Qataris, and Israelis

ISIL/Al Nusra was also enriching itself from ransom payments for hostages, money mostly received from Qatar. Qatar paid ransom payments to Al Nusra-ISIL units for some Syrian nuns and captured Lebanese Army soldiers. Meanwhile, Saudi Arabia was training so-called Free Syrian Army "moderates" the Assad government. In the past, the Saudis conducted such training in order to radicalize Sunni Muslim volunteers for the Syrian civil war and funnel them to ISIL units in Syria and Iraq.

Israel was also reported to be transporting Al Nusra/ISIL terrorists across the Golan frontier into Israel, ostensibly for medical treatment, but also for intelligence and other military training. Netanyahu's Twitter statement that "Hamas is ISIS" was a crude attempt to confuse those in the West who did not understand what was at the root of the ISIL insurrection.

The Wall Street Journal, which provided the government of Israeli Prime Minister Netanyahu with unending editorial support, reported that Israel provided logistical support in Syria to Al Qaeda and its affiliate, *Jabhat al-Nusra*. The paper reported that Al-Nusra "hasn't bothered Israel since seizing the border area last summer" along the Golan Heights. In fact, the core Al Qaeda and its official branches never "bothered" Israel.[17] Israel provided medical assistance to some 2000 Syrians, a number of them members of the Nusra Front and Al Qaeda.

France was also not an idle bystander to the creation and nurturing of ISIL. Terrorist Boubaker El-Hakim, a French national of Tunisian descent, had close ties to French intelligence. There was yet another ISIL affiliate operative who worked for the French external intelligence service, *Direction générale de la sécurité extérieure* – DGSE. That ex-French agent, David Drugeon, actually became a leader of the Khorasan Group in Syria.

On October 5, 2014, McClatchy news service reported that Drugeon "defected" from DGSE to Al Qaeda. Although Western intelligence finds it useful to separate ISIL or the Islamic State, the Khorasan Group, Al Qaeda, and the Al Nusra Front, on the Syrian and Iraqi battlefields these groups fight under the same command and same black and white jihadist banner. [18]

Drugeon was raised Catholic in Vannes, Brittany. He allegedly converted to Salafist Islam and took the name of Daoud. He was known by the nickname "Français d'Al Qaïda." Afterwards, Drugeon is said to have received military-like training from a civilian French government organization.[19] The quarters that immediately questioned the veracity of the McClatchy report were all neo-conservative in nature, with the loudest shouting coming from a very noisy neo-con cell at the U.S. Naval War College whose job appeared to be to attack journalists who reported information that ran counter to the memes issued by the neocon-controlled press. The McClatchy report was also attacked by the Foundation for the Defense of Democracies, a virtual Mossad front in Washington; the pro-business *L'Opinion* of France; and the Rothschild banking family-linked *L'Express* of Paris.

Intelligence observers in Europe believed that Drugeon was placed by DGSE within the ranks of Khorasan to give it as much gravitas as that already possessed by ISIL, in order to justify greater Western military involvement in Syria. In fact, the U.S. Director of National Intelligence James Clapper said Khorasan was as "great a threat to the homeland" as ISIL. The U.S. Central Command stated that

---

[17] Yaroslav Trofimov, "Al Qaeda a Lesser Evil? Syria War Pulls U.S., Israel Apart," *The Wall Street Journal*, March 12, 2015.

[18] McClatchy News, "Sources: U.S. air strikes in Syria targeted French agent who defected to al Qaida," October 5, 2014.

[19] Ibid.

Khorasan included seasoned core fighters who took part in operations for Al Qaeda and the Al Nusra Front. Drugeon reportedly provided Khorasan with advanced bomb-making capabilities.

Israel's military and intelligence services also provided assistance to Al Nusra in Syria and ISIL in Iraq. Hakem al-Zameli, the chairman of the Iraqi Parliament's National Security and Defense Committee, stated that Iraq's armed forces shot down two British planes that were carrying weapons to ISIL in Anbar province, the same province where Israeli commandos have been witnessed transferring weapons to ISIL forces. Al-Zameli also said that his committee is receiving daily reports from Anbar province about successive U.S. coalition planes airdropping weapons and other materials for ISIL in areas held by the jihadist group.[20]

Khalaf Tarmouz, the head of the Anbar Provincial Council said local officials have discovered U.S., European, and Israeli weapons from the areas liberated from ISIL in the Al-Bagdadi region. The Iraqi government also revealed that U.S. coalition forces airdropped weapons to support ISIL in Salahuddin, Al-Anbar and Diyala provinces. Member of Parliament Majid al-Gharawi said he was aware of U.S. airdrops of weapons for ISIL in Salahuddin and other Iraqi provinces.

Al-Zameli said, "The US drops weapons for the ISIL on the excuse of not knowing about the whereabouts of the ISIL positions, and it is trying to distort the reality with its allegations." He said evidence was provided by Iraqi army officers and other Iraqi forces.

Iranian Brigadier General Massoud Jazayeri confirmed the Iraqi government reports. He said, "The U.S. and the so-called anti-ISIL coalition claim that they have launched a campaign against this terrorist and criminal group – while supplying them with weapons, food and medicine in Jalawla region [in Diyala Governorate].[21]

Western intelligence links to ISIL began to be systematically exposed around the world. Chechen President Ramzan Kadyrov declared that ISIL's leader, Ibrahim Samarrai, aka "Abu Bakr al-Baghdadi," was a Central Intelligence Agency operative who received financial backing from Western intelligence services. From reports coming from Iraq and Syria, the links between the violent jihadists and their CIA, MI-6, DGSE, and Mossad overseers were becoming abundantly clear.

---

[20] Fars News Agency, "Iraqi Army Downs 2 UK Planes Carrying Weapons for ISIL," February 23, 2015.
[21] *Ibid.*

It was revealed in May 2015 that the U.S.-trained commander of Tajikistan's OMON Special Forces, Colonel Gulmurod Khalimov, had defected to ISIL to serve as one of the group's top field commanders in Syria. After his defection, Khalimov said in a video, "Listen, you American pigs, I've been three times to America, and I saw how you train fighters to kill Muslims . . . God willing, I will come with this weapon to your cities, your homes, and we will kill you."[22] . Khalimov was reportedly trained by U.S. Special Operations forces, Blackwater, and the CIA during a number of official visits to the United States

The leader of Lebanon's Druze Progressive Socialist Party, Walid Jumblatt, who was always an erratic on-and-off supporter of Israel, concluded an agreement with the Al Nusra Front and its Al Qaeda affiliate in Syria. Jumblatt concluded the agreement even though his fellow Druze in Idlib, Syria were given an ultimatum by ISIL to convert to Wahhabi Islam and destroy their shrines, mausoleums, and religious icons or face execution. Jumblatt is reported by the Lebanese press to have arranged for the forced conversions of the Idlib Druze in exchange for their lives using the offices of the United Arab Emirates.[23]

It was also reported in the Lebanese press that Israel helped arrange for contacts, using Jordanian intelligence interlocutors, between Al Nusra/Al Qaeda and the Syrian Druze. Israel offered military and intelligence support to the Syrian Druze if they attacked Syrian government forces and their Lebanese Hezbollah allies in Syria.

---

[22] Ishan Tharoor, "The U.S.-trained commander of Tajikistan's special forces has joined the Islamic State," The Washington Post, May 28, 2015.
[23] *Daily Star*, "Jumblatt, Nusra reach agreement on Idlib's Druze: report," March 2, 2015.

Other Israeli fingerprints on ISIL:

The Israeli press reported that gardeners in the northern Israeli city of Nazareth Illit discovered a bag containing about 25 new black-and-white ISIL flags. The discovery of the flags further implicated the Israeli government in providing not only military and logistical support to ISIL, but propaganda support, as well.

Turkish foreign minister Mevlut Cavusoglu revealed that Turkish authorities arrested a foreign intelligence agent, believed to be an asset of the Canadian Security and Intelligence Service (CSIS), who was charged with helping three British schoolgirls travel from Britain through Turkey and then into Syria to join ISIL. Under the Stephen Harper government, Canadian intelligence was ordered to assist Mossad in all matters requested by the Israelis. The arrested agent was Mohammed Mehmet Rashid, aka "Doctor Mehmet Rashid," Mohammed al Rashid, and Mohammad Al Rashed, who reported to Bruno Saccomani, the Canadian ambassador to Jordan and Iraq. Saccomani is a former Royal Canadian Mounted Police (RCMP) officer who was the head of Harper's personal security detail until he was appointed ambassador to Amman. Saccomani was criticized by other RCMP officers for his "bullying" tactics. The appointment was roundly criticized by the Canadian opposition because Saccomani had no diplomatic experience. Al Rashid met the three British school girls at Gaziantep near the Syrian border and personally delivered them into ISIL hands in Syria. Saccomani served as the RCMP liaison officer at the Canadian embassy in Rome in 1997 where he developed a close working relationship with Israeli intelligence and law enforcement officials.

Russian President Vladimir Putin's aide Alexander Prokhanov charged in December 2014 that Mossad was training ISIL's leadership.

News reports from around the Middle East revealed that Abu Bakr Al Baghdad, the self-proclaimed ISIL "caliph," received a year of intensive language and Islamic theology training from his Mossad handlers.

Adrian Kaba, a member of Sweden's ruling Social Democratic Party who served on the Malmo City Council and the regional government, wrote in 2014 that Mossad provided training to ISIL. Kaba wrote on his Facebook page that "ISIS is being trained by the Israeli Mossad. Muslims are not waging war, they are being used as pawns by other peoples' game."

Israeli foreign minister Avigdor Lieberman suggested ISIL-style beheadings for Israeli Arabs suspected of supporting terrorism.

Prince Bandar bin Sultan, the godfather behind the creation of ISIL, returned to an influential position advising the late King Abdullah after having earlier been sacked as Saudi intelligence chief in April 2014. Bandar's new title was "adviser to the King and his special envoy." Bandar had never actually left the Saudi inner circle. Even after being sacked as intelligence chief, Bandar retained his position as secretary general of the Saudi National Security Council, a position similar to that held by Susan Rice as the White House National Security Adviser and director of the National Security Council.

The House of Saud was a major bank-roller of ISIL since the beginning of the insurgent group's role in Syria's civil war. The Al Nusra Front (Jabhat al-Nusra), on the other hand, was mainly funded by Qatar. The Al Nusra Front, far from being a rival to ISIL, pledged its support for the group as its forces spread across northern and western Iraq.

The actual aim of Saudi Arabia was to destabilize Iraq and Syria, hoping that the Iraqi Shi'a-dominated government and Bashar al Assad's government in Damascus would be overthrown and replaced with radical Sunni regimes beholden to the Saudis.

Bandar had longstanding ties to Jihadist terrorism. On a pre-Sochi Olympics trip to Moscow, he offered a lucrative weapons deal if Russia would cease its support for Assad. Bandar also told Putin that if Russia rejected Saudi Arabia's offer, Saudi-backed Islamist terrorists in the Caucasus region would be free to launch terrorist attacks on the Winter Olympics in Sochi. Putin reportedly ordered Bandar out of his office in the Kremlin. There are also reports that Saudi-financed Islamist terrorists from Chechnya and Dagestan were active fighting against Russian-speaking separatists in eastern Ukraine. In some cases, Islamist terrorists have joined Israeli paramilitary units in Ukraine in support of the Kiev government's military actions against eastern Ukraine. In Syria, there have been reports of Mossad coordination with ISIL units in attacks against Syrian government forces, including in the region north of the Golan Heights.

Bandar's name was reportedly contained in the classified 28 pages from the Joint Congressional 9/11 Inquiry report on Saudi Arabia's role in the 9/11 attack. Attempts to have the 28 pages declassified met with strong opposition from Brennan and the CIA, as well as the Obama White House and Saudi and Israeli lobbies in Washington. Former Senator Bob Graham (D-FL), who chaired the Senate Intelligence Committee at the time the report was written, called for the 28 pages to be made public. A reliable source reported that

Graham was cold-shouldered when he visited the White House in 2014 to press for full disclosure. Graham was shuffled off to meet with a low-level White House staffer instead of any influential White House policy makers.

DIA exposes Western backing for ISIL

A formerly SECRET NOFORN (No Foreign Dissemination) message, dated August 5, 2012, to the Defense Intelligence Agency (DIA) from a redacted U.S. government agency, provided more evidence that ISIL was a construct of U.S. intelligence.

The message, declassified as the result of a Freedom of Information Act request submitted by Judicial Watch, a conservative organization, indicates that the intelligence on ISIL was "not finally evaluated," which means it was not sanitized and editorialized by the political operatives within the U.S. intelligence community.

The message released was unusual in that some of the action and information "addees" were redacted, which was not normally the case with declassified message traffic, whether they originated with the Defense Department, State Department, or U.S. intelligence agencies.

The message led off with the following: "The Salafist, the Muslim Brotherhood, and AQI [Al Qaeda in Iraq] are the major forces driving the insurgency in Iraq." The message goes on to state: "The West, Gulf countries, and Turkey support the [Syrian] opposition; while Russia, China, and Iran support the regime." The "regime" was the government of Syrian President Bashar al-Assad.

The message also stated: "AQI supported the Syrian opposition from the beginning, both ideologically and through the media . . . and conducted a number of operations in several under the name of Jaish al Nusra (Victorious Army), one of its affiliates."

There was also a direct reference to the similarity of Western support for the Syrian and Iraqi jihadists and those who emerged in Libya following the overthrow of Muammar el-Qaddafi. This support was directed to internationally-supported "safe havens" harboring the jihadist and Salafist forces: "Opposition forces are trying to control the eastern areas (Hasaka and Der Zor), adjacent to the western Iraqi provinces (Mosul and Anbar), in addition to neighboring Turkish borders. *Western countries, the Gulf countries and Turkey are supporting these efforts* [emphasis added]. This hypothesis is most likely in accordance with the data from recent events, which will help prepare safe havens under international sheltering, similar to what transpired in Libya when Benghazi was chosen as the command center of the temporary government." What the message does not state is that the "safe havens" in Syria, Iraq, and Benghazi were the locations where the Islamic State and its allies declared a caliphate (the Islamic caliphate in Syria and Iraq) and an emirate (the Emirate of Derna in eastern Libya).

The operative paragraph stated that the "supporting powers to the opposition" wanted to establish a "declared or undeclared Salafist principality in eastern Syria (Hasaka and Der Zor), and this is <u>exactly</u> what the supporting powers [Western countries, the Gulf countries and Turkey] want, in order to isolate the Syrian regime, which is considered the strategic depth of the Shia expansion (Iraq and Iran)."

C. IF THE SITUATION UNRAVELS THERE IS THE POSSIBILITY OF ESTABLISHING A DECLARED OR UNDECLARED SALAFIST PRINCIPALITY IN EASTERN SYRIA (HASAKA AND DER ZOR), AND THIS IS EXACTLY WHAT THE SUPPORTING POWERS TO THE OPPOSITION WANT, IN ORDER TO ISOLATE THE SYRIAN REGIME, WHICH IS CONSIDERED THE STRATEGIC DEPTH OF THE SHIA EXPANSION (IRAQ AND IRAN).

The Western powers – the United States, Britain, France, and, more importantly, Israel – working in concert with the Gulf countries [Saudi Arabia, Qatar, United Arab Emirates, Kuwait, and Bahrain], as well as Turkey, according to U.S. intelligence, created ISIL to destroy the Shia-dominated nations of Syria and Iraq. The fall of Palmyra in Syria and Ramadi in Iraq were a result of this conspiracy of "supporting powers." The civil war in Yemen that saw the very same "supporting powers," including Egypt, provide military forces to fight the Shi'a-aligned Houthi rebels was, like the civil wars in Syria and Iraq, of U.S. Saudi, Israeli, and Turkish design. Ultimately, Iran was the ultimate target for the "supporting powers" of ISIL and its allies.

While ISIL forces ransacked and destroyed Shi'a shrines and mosques in Iraq and Syria, Saudi war planes leveled Shi'a mosques and revered buildings in Yemen. In another example of how the Saudis and ISIL are on the same page, it was a Saudi military checkpoint that allowed an ISIL terrorist unit to enter the town of Qadih in eastern Saudi Arabia to bomb a Shi'a mosque in May 2015. There was not one criticism of the Saudi regime in the official statement issued by ISIL taking credit for the deadly blast at the mosque. And of course, the ISIL statement, as usual, was discovered by the SITE Institute, Mossad's intelligence operation that spins alleged jihadist communiqués to the international media.

There were also suspicious links between ISIL and the Iranian exiled terrorist group Mojahedin-e-Khalq (MEK) through CIA and Israeli Mossad interlocutors. These links included personal contacts between the husband-and-wife leadership of the MEK, Massoud and Maryam Rajavi, and the senior leadership of ISIL. These contacts were reportedly authorized by ISIL's self-proclaimed "caliph" Abu Bakr al-

Baghdadi. ISIL and the MEK also jointly approached the Baluchi terrorist group *Jundallah*, which operated in western Pakistan, on conducting joint terrorist operations against Iran. These contacts were facilitated by Saudi Arabia, the CIA, and Mossad.

MEK paramilitary units continued to be based at Camp Liberty, also known as Camp Hurriya, to the west of Baghdad, where they were protected by CIA contractor personnel. Iranian intelligence was well aware of contacts between the MEK and ISIL units fighting in the western environs of Baghdad and in some cases witnessed MEK and ISIL guerrillas and CIA contractors involved in joint operations against Iraqi army personnel.

The CIA-supported MEK had been described as a "cult" by members who managed to escape its control. There were credible reports from witnesses concerning torture by the MEK of 3000 internees at Camp Liberty. MEK members were moved to Camp Liberty by the United States from the group's former Iraqi base at Camp Ashraf. Named after Massoud Rajavi's first wife, Camp Ashraf was once supported by Iraqi President Saddam Hussein.

ISIL was also deemed a non-Islamic "cult" by a number of Middle Eastern intelligence services who cited the large number of French Jews who have joined the organization. On October 14, *Ha'aretz* reported the following: "There are a number of Jews among the more than 1,000 French citizens who have joined the Islamic State, a French government official told Israel's Channel 2 news."[24] ISIL also attracted Buddhists from Japan, Hindus from India, Catholics from Italy, and Protestants from Canada and Australia as recruits. Some of them were so-called recent "converts" to Islam while others had not converted.

Both the MEK and ISIL hold dissident members hostage against their will. The MEK, like ISIL, received training, weapons, and funding from the Mossad. The Israel Lobby in the U.S. arranged for its many political supporters, including former New York Mayor Rudolph Giuliani, former Vermont Governor Howard Dean, former Pennsylvania Governor Ed Rendell, former Obama national security adviser General James Jones, former New Jersey senator Robert Torricelli, former CIA directors James Woolsey and Porter Goss, former U.S. ambassador to the UN John Bolton, and Harvard professor Alan Dershowitz, to publicly support the goals of the MEK. In 2012, Secretary of State Hillary Clinton de-listed the MEK as a

---

[24] *Ha'aretz*, "More Jews Have Joined Islamic State, French Official Says," October 14, 2014.

foreign terrorist organization and permitted the group to re-open its office in Washington, DC. The MEK office in the National Press Building was originally closed by the Bush administration in 2003.

The current MEK-ISIL alliance made all the aforementioned political notables witting or unwitting enablers of ISIL operations in Iraq, Syria, and, reportedly, operations inside Iran with the assistance of MEK units.

The CIA's and Pentagon's support for a terrorist grouping like ISIL and its allies is not new in American history. The Pentagon's crazed scheme to launch terrorist attacks on U.S. and allied targets in the early 1960s and blame them on Fidel Castro's Cuba – Operation Northwoods – is legendary in the annals of U.S. state-supported terrorism. Other examples include the CIA's Operation Gladio that saw right-wing groups carry out deadly terrorist attacks in Europe during the 1970s and 80s that were blamed on leftist groups and the CIA's Operation Phoenix that saw the U.S. randomly assassinate South Vietnamese village leaders and Buddhist clerics.

Former U.S. commander in Iraq and director of the CIA General David Petraeus called for the U.S. to ally with Al Qaeda against ISIL. Many CIA veterans understand that there is no real difference between the rank and file members of Al Qaeda and ISIL, and they know that Al Qaeda in Iraq morphed into ISIL in both Iraq and Syria. The Ivy League denizen Petraeus was personally involved in training Iraqi Sunni insurgents during his time in Iraq. Ironically, the two training programs that saw U.S. weapons and training provided to the nascent Al Qaeda and ISIL forces were code named IVY SERPENT and IVY CYCLONE. These covert operations, in addition to COPPER GREEN, which identified potential Sunni agents of influence for the United States inside the Abu Ghraib prison and other Iraqi detention centers, created the two al-Baghdadis.

To quote cartoonist Walt Kelly from his famous Pogo comic strip, "We have met the enemy and he is us."

Further Articles

by Wayne Madsen
Originally Published by the Strategic Culture Foundation

***

New Saudi King Was Major Supporter of Al Qaeda

January 25, 2015. The new king of Saudi Arabia, Salman bin Abdulaziz al Saud, the half-brother of King Abdullah, who died in his early 90s of complications from pneumonia, is expected to rule with a more Wahhabist-oriented religious bent and concentrate on limiting cautious political reforms started by Abdullah. Salman is also expected to devote his energies to increasing Saudi national security. Salman's devotion to Saudi security is hypocritical at best due to his past support for Al Qaeda, including some of the individuals implicated in the 9/11 attack on the United States. It is Salman's involvement with financing 9/11 and other terrorists that will likely reinforce the Obama administration's refusal to declassify 28 missing pages from the 2002 Senate Intelligence Committee's report on the intelligence failures surrounding the attack. As the then-governor of Riyadh, Salman's name likely appears as a "big fish" in the redacted 28 pages from the Senate report.

On the surface, Salman will not govern much differently than his predecessor in affairs of oil politics and national security. Salman will be assisted by his son, Prince Mohammed bin Salman, the minister of defense and the chief of the royal court. Mohammed was the chief adviser to his father when Salman served as the governor of Riyadh province. Prince Mohammed became defense minister when his father acceded to the throne upon the death of Abdullah.

The other chief adviser to Salman will be Mohammed bin Nayef, the minister of the interior since 2012 and the current deputy Crown Prince and Second Deputy Prime Minister. Nayef, a nephew of King Salman, is second in line to the throne after Crown Prince Muqrin bin Abdulaziz al Saud. Muqrin was the head of the Saudi Mukhabarat al-A'amah, the Saudi intelligence agency, from 2005 to 2012.

In 2006, Saudi democratic opposition leaders in Britain fingered Salman, the then-governor of Riyadh province, as providing material assistance to Al Qaeda forces operating in Afghanistan before and after 9/11. The opposition revealed that Al Qaeda members routinely traveled through Riyadh on their way to Pakistan and then to Taliban-ruled regions of Afghanistan. These Saudi insiders also reported that Salman's governor's office arranged for cash payments, hotels, and air fares for the Al Qaeda members.

There is little doubt that Salman's activities on behalf of Al Qaeda were known to the Central Intelligence Agency (CIA), which approved of the Saudi pipeline of providing Arab guerrillas to Afghanistan's mujahedin forces since the early days of Langley's involvement in the jihadist campaign to oust Afghanistan's socialist and secular government from power. Shortly before his suspicious death in Scotland in 2005, former British Foreign Secretary Robin Cook wrote in The Guardian that "Al Qaeda" was a CIA database of mercenaries, financiers, and interlocutors used by the CIA to fight the Soviets in Afghanistan: "Throughout the 80s he [Osama bin Laden] was armed by the CIA and funded by the Saudis to wage jihad against the Russian occupation of Afghanistan. Al-Qaida [sic], literally 'the database,' was originally the computer file of the thousands of mujahedin who were recruited and trained with help from the CIA to defeat the Russians".

From the accounts of the Saudi opposition and Cook, it is inconceivable that Salman was unaware of the activities of his governor's staff in Riyadh.

When a Saudi prince and a reputed relative of King Salman's chief adviser Prince Mohammed bin Nayef, who was also named Nayef, was caught by France trafficking in cocaine in 1999, the Saudi Interior Ministry informed Paris in 2000 that if France brought criminal charges against the minor prince Nayef, a lucrative $7 billion radar defense contract, Project SBGDP ("Garde Frontiere"), with the French firm Thales would be canceled. The details are found in a Confidential French diplomatic cable dated February 21, 2000. The subject of the cable was an audience between French officials and Saudi Interior Minister Prince Nayef in the case of a Saudi plane suspected of trafficking in narcotics ("Prince Nayef, ministre saoudien de l'interieure. Affaire de l'avion saoudien soupçonné d'avoir servi à un trafic de stupéfiants.") The cable was sent by the technical adviser in the French ministry of the interior François Gouyette to the French justice ministry and the French embassy in Riyadh. Gouyette became the French ambassador to the United Arab Emirates in 2001.

The cocaine trafficked by Nayef was, according to a Confidential U.S. Drug Enforcement Administration (DEA) document, being used to fund Al Qaeda in Afghanistan. The cash that was paid to terrorist recruits passing through Riyadh was obtained by the Interior Ministry from the drug proceeds coffers held in secret bank accounts. The CIA was aware of and encouraged the off-the-books payments to the Al Qaeda recruits, just as it is doing today with the Al Qaeda recruits being emptied from Saudi prisons and paid by Saudi government interlocutors.

In 1999, the DEA broke open a major conspiracy involving Prince Nayef's Colombian cocaine smuggling from Venezuela to support some "future intention" involving Koranic prophecy. The DEA operations were contained in a "Declassification of a Secret DEA 6 Paris Country Office" memorandum dated June 26, 2000. In June 1999, 808 kilograms of cocaine were seized in Paris. At the same time, the DEA was conducting a major investigation of the Medellin drug cartel called Operation Millennium.

Through an intercepted fax, the Bogota Country Office of the DEA learned of the Paris cocaine seizure and linked the drug smuggling operation to the Saudis. The DEA investigation centered around Saudi Prince Nayef al Saud, whose alias was "El Principe" (the Prince). Nayef's full name is Nayef (or Nayif) bin Fawwaz al-Shaalan al-Saud. In pursuit of his international drug deals, Nayef traveled in his own Boeing 727 and used his diplomatic status to avoid customs checks. The DEA report stated Nayef studied at the University of Miami, Florida, owned a bank in Switzerland, spoke eight languages, was heavily invested in Venezuela's petroleum industry, regularly visited the United States, and traveled with millions of dollars of U.S. currency. Nayef was also invested in Colombia's petroleum industry.

Nayef was also reported to have met with drug cartel members in Marbella, Spain, where the Saudi royal family maintains a huge palatial residence. The report states that when a group of cartel members traveled to Riyadh to meet Nayef, "they were picked up in a Rolls Royce automobile belonging to Nayef, and driven to the Riyadh Holiday Inn hotel. The next day they were met by Nayef and his brother [believed to be named Saul [sic] [His twin brother is Prince Saud. Nayef's older brother, Prince Nawaf, is married to King Abdullah's daughter].)... The second day they all traveled to the desert in terrain vehicles [Hummers]. During this desert trip they discussed narcotics trafficking. "UN" [the DEA informant] and Nayef agreed to conduct the 2,000 kilogram cocaine shipment, which would be delivered to Caracas, VZ, by UN's people, where Nayef would facilitate the cocaine's transport to Paris, France. Nayef explained he would utilize his 727 jet airliner, under Diplomatic cover, to transport the cocaine.

Nayef told "UN" that he could transport up to 20,000 kilograms of cocaine in his jet airliner, and propositioned "UN" to conduct 10-20,000 kilogram shipments in the future. "UN" wondered why Nayef, supposedly a devout Muslim, would be involved with drugs. Nayef's response in light of what is now known about Saudi funding of terrorism, is worth a close perusal. During the Riyadh meeting, Nayef responded to "UN's" question by stating that "he is a strict advocate of the Muslim Corran [sic]." "UN" stated, "Nayef does not drink, smoke, or violate any of the Corran's [sic] teachings." "UN" asked Nayef why he [Nayef] wanted to sell cocaine and Nayef stated that the world is already doomed and that he had been authorized by God to sell drugs. Nayef stated that "UN" would later learn of Nayef's true intentions for trafficking narcotics although Nayef would not comment further. The Saudi prince's drug smuggling operation was smashed by the DEA and French police in October 1999.

Drug money laundering in support of Al Qaeda terrorists in Afghanistan and Pakistan, a strict interpretation of the Koran in the future governance of Saudi Arabia, the return of the feared "mutaween" religious police, and a crackdown on legitimate internal dissent in Saudi Arabia: this is the legacy and governance style that King Salman brings to Saudi Arabia.

Christians Fleeing the Pseudo-Islamist Blood Cult of the "Islamic State"

April 8, 2015. There's not many groups that the pseudo-Islamist blood cult known as the "Islamic State" or Islamic State of Iraq and the Levant (ISIL) have not targeted for genocide. However, the Middle East's ancient Christian community has fared worse under Islamic State occupation than have Syrian and Iraqi Kurds, Shi'a Muslims, Syrian Alawites, moderate Sunni Muslims, and Palestinian refugees. Only the Yazidis have suffered the same degree of merciless genocide by the Saudi- and Israeli-backed Islamic State forces as have the Christians. Thousands of Christians have fled their historic cities, towns, and monastic communities for safety in other countries, outside the rule of the self-proclaimed Islamic "caliphate" of ISIL, Abu Bakr al-Baghdadi.

One of the first Christian communities to flee the ISIL "blood cult" marauders was that of Raqqa, Syria. Raqqa was the first major city to fall to ISIL after the Israeli Mossad and U.S. Central Intelligence Agency permitted arms allegedly destined for the almost-nonexistent "Free Syrian Army" to falls into the hands of ISIL and their Jabhat al-Nusra allies. Although Christians represented only one percent of Raqqa's 300,000 population, almost all fled or were killed after ISIL burned down and defaced churches and imposed a confiscatory "dhimma" religious tax on Christians of 17 grams of gold from each Christian male. In all, a half million Syrian Christians have fled their country thanks to Saudi, Western, and Israeli support for ISIL and affiliated radicals.

The Saudis and Qataris also helped finance the so-called "Islamist" state juggernaut in Syria, which eventually poured over the border into western and northern Iraq and immediately posed a threat to Assyrian Christians and other religious and ethnic minorities.

The United States and, in particular, the Central Intelligence Agency under its fanatically pro-Saudi director, John Brennan, has, in addition to permitting weapons and financial aid to reach ISIL and allied forces in Syria and Iraq, provided intelligence, materiel, and propaganda support to the Saudi-led coalition battling Houthi and patriotic Yemeni forces in that nation's multi-sided civil war. This has placed the United States on the same side as ISIL/Al Qaeda forces in South and North Yemen that have received covert assistance from the Saudis in carrying out horrific terrorist attacks upon the Houthis and members of the Zaidi Islamic sect who support them. Although Yemen's Christian population is very small, the threat posed by ISIL and its allies to foreign workers in Yemen, including Christians, prompted their mass evacuation from the country, mainly through the port of Aden.

After the ISIL scourge crossed from Syria into Iraq, many, armed with U.S. weapons delivered to the "Free Syrian Army" by the CIA and Pentagon, set out to attack the Christians of northern Iraq. As a bonus, ISIL guerrillas captured U.S. weapons from deserting Iraqi troops. In June 2014, Mosul was the first major Christian population center to fall to ISIL, prompting most of the city's 80,000 Christians to flee the region. ISIL set about to destroy churches of the Chaldean Catholic archdiocese and the Assyrian Orthodox diocese in Mosul. The Assyrians speak Aramaic, the language spoken by Jesus as his primary tongue. In fact, on his visit to Palestine and Israel, Pope Francis schooled an arrogant Israeli Prime Minister Binyamin Netanyahu, who believed he knew otherwise, on the fact that Aramaic was Jesus's main language and that Hebrew was a second tongue.

There were three large Assyrian Christian denominations active in Mosul before the city's fall to the Islamist cultists: the Assyrian Church of the East (known as "Nestorian"), the Syriac Orthodox Church (called "Jacobite"), and the Chaldean Church of Babylon (Roman Catholic rite). Priceless religious artifacts were smashed and burned by the crypto-cultist "caliphate" marauders. In July 2014, ISIL leaders proudly proclaimed that Mosul had been "cleansed" of Christians. There was nary a peep from Israel about the religious cleansing of Mosul even though its propaganda machine conveniently ensures that the Nazi cleansing of Jews from Europe receives front page attention every time Israel faces criticism for its own atrocities against the Palestinians. Nor did Israel's friends in the "Christian Zionist" community in the United States raise any alarms over the pogrom by ISIL and its Saudi and Qatari financiers against the Christians of northern Iraq and Syria.

By February 2015, ISIL had cemented ties with like-minded cultists in Libya, many of whom were propelled into power by the NATO intervention in that nation and the bloody overthrow of Muammar Qaddafi. Thanks to the efforts of French "philosopher" Bernard-Henri Levy, who shuttled between rebel-held areas of Benghazi and Netanyahu's office in Jerusalem, the most radical Islamist jihadi factions took over power from Qaddafi in and around Benghazi. These factions ultimately swore allegiance to the Islamic State, which, in February 2015 carried out the mass beheading of 21 Egyptian Coptic Christian oil workers on a Mediterranean beach near Tripoli. That same month, ISIL terrorists kidnapped 300 Assyrian Christians in Iraq, including a number of children, from their villages along the Khabur River.

The kidnapping sent some 1300 additional Assyrians fleeing for their lives from the area.

On March 15, 2015, inspired and funded by the same Saudi Wahhabist elements who provide assistance to ISIL and its like-minded blood-lusting allies, the Pakistani Taliban bombed two churches in Lahore, killing over a dozen Christian faithful. Four days later, ISIL detonated the 4th Century Mar Benham Christian monastery in Bakhdida, near Mosul. The 1600 year-old building was built by Assyrian king Senchareb and was a UNESCO-protected World Heritage Site.

As ISIL forces approached the outer edges of Baghdad, many of the 100,000 Christians remaining in the city prepared to evacuate. Iraq's Christians thrived before the U.S. invasion and occupation and even counted one of their own, Tariq Aziz, as Iraq's foreign minister and deputy prime minister under Saddam Hussein. Rather than demolish Christian churches, Saddam used part of Iraq's oil revenue to repair many Iraqi churches worn down by time and neglect.

On April 3, 2015, Maundy Thursday, when Christians were celebrating Jesus's Last Supper, Islamist guerrillas of the Somali-based and ISIL-aligned Al Shabaab group, stormed into the campus of Garissa University in Kenya and massacred 147 Christian students. The guerrillas ensured that the Christians were singled out from other students before they were executed. Meanwhile, ISIL supporters within the Nigerian group Boko Haram continued to target Christians in that beleaguered nation.

To those like the CIA's Brennan, the Israeli benefactors of ISIL/Nusra in Syria and Iraq, and others who turn a blind eye to ISIL's war against Christianity, Pope Francis, in his Good Friday message, had a simple but dire warning: "We risk, all of us, the institutions and the people of the Western world, to be Pontius Pilate who wash their hands of such atrocities". However, many Wahhabists, Muslim Brotherhood members, and right-wing Israelis take pleasure in the fact that ISIL has declared Christianity, not Judaism or Shi'a Islam, to be its "Number 1 enemy". This is spelled out in the ISIL propaganda booklet titled "Dabiq".

ISIL propaganda has depicted ISIL's black flag flying over St. Peter's Basilica in Vatican City. ISIL says it will eventually conquer Italy, Spain, the Balkans, and Austria. There is only one way to stamp out the scourge of ISIL forever, and that is to ensure that the governments of Syria and Iraq, as well as the exiled remnants of supporters of Qaddafi of Libya, see to it that the only flag torn down and replaced is that of the Saudi monarchy which flies over Riyadh, Jeddah, Mecca, and Medina. With that flag gone, the flags of ISIL and Al Qaeda will never fly over another church in the Middle East or anywhere.

ISIL: Made in Langley

June 26, 2015. It is becoming more and more apparent that the Islamic State for Iraq and the Levant (ISIL), or "Daesh" as it is known in Arabic, or ISIS – the Islamic State of Iraq and al-Sham -- preferred by Israel supporters because of the uncomforting similarity between "Israel" and "ISIL" – is part of another Central Intelligence Agency operation to artificially create a new "strategy of tensions" for the Eurasian and African land masses.

Yet another example of ISIL's non-Islamic nature has been witnessed in the ancient Syrian city of Palmyra – the blowing up of the tomb of Mohammad Bin Ali, a descendant of the Prophet Mohammed's cousin Imam Ali, by the brigands and mercenaries of ISIL. ISIL's true goal is to eradicate the Arab and pre-Arab history of the Middle East with one major exception. There have been virtually no reports of important antiquities sacred to the Zionists having been destroyed by ISIL in either Syria or Iraq. The major targets for the ISIL demolition teams have been Sumerian, Akkadian, Babylonian, Roman, Assyrian, Persian, Alawite, Druze, Turkmen, Yazidi, Parthian, Christian, Shi'a, and Sufi (the other major tomb destroyed in Palmyra was the tomb of Nizar Abu Bahaa Eddine, a Sufi scholar who lived 500 years ago). ISIL destroyed the Tomb of Yunus (Jonah) Mosque in Iraq not because it honored the Jewish patriarch Jonah but because it was a mosque.

The alleged tomb of the Jewish prophet Daniel destroyed by ISIL in Mosul is but one of six Daniel tombs located in Iraq, Iran, and Uzbekistan. The Talmud, the Jewish book from which the Zionists obtain most of their geo-political inspiration, strictly prohibits any images of faces, but permits owning images of faces created by non-Jews. Although ISIL and Talmudists are on the same page on destroying sculptures, tiles, and paintings depicting people, the Talmud's exception that allows Jews to own images created by non-Jews has resulted in a lucrative black market for antiquities stolen by ISIL and sold through brokers in Tel Aviv, Amsterdam, and Geneva.

It is becoming clear that ISIL, from the very beginning, was a construct of the CIA and its pro-Saudi and pro-Israeli director, John Brennan; Israel's Mossad, which has ensured that Israeli targets are exempt from ISIL attack; and Saudi Arabia, which actually permitted ISIL attacks against two Shi'a mosques, one in the village of al-Qadeeh and the other in Dammam, in the Eastern Province, where Shi'as have a majority over Wahhabist Sunnis. In Iraq and Syria, U.S. and Israeli weapons have been seen by eyewitnesses being transferred to ISIL and forces of its allies, including the Al Nusra Front in Syria. Saudi bank cash receipts have been found in abandoned ISIL headquarters in both Syria and Iraq. The ISIL attacks on the Shi'as of Saudi Arabia are believed by many to be warnings by the unholy alliance of Washington, Tel Aviv, and Riyadh against predominantly Shi'a Iran.

Further Articles

From the terrorist Gladio "stay behind" network of fascists, which carried out terrorist attacks in Europe in the 1970s and 80s that were blamed on leftist irregulars, to the grand alliance of terrorists from Angola's UNITA, the Afghan mujaheddin, the Nicaraguan contras, Laotian Hmongs who, under American auspices, met in 1985 in Jamba, Angola, the CIA has historically found that terrorist groups make advantageous allies. The CIA clandestinely and illegally violated two U.S. laws, the Clark and Boland Amendments, respectively, to support Angolan and Nicaraguan terrorists.

ISIL now serves as an important CIA, Saudi, and Israeli asset against common foes like Iran. ISIL has made no secret of its desire to bring the death and destruction it has visited upon Syria and Iraq into the heart of Iran. The destabilization of Iran by sponsoring terrorist attacks in Iran and against Iranian targets abroad has long been the modus operandi of the U.S., Israel, and Saudi Arabia, acting mostly through the anti-Tehran Mojahedin-e-Khalq (MEK) and Baluchi separatists based in Pakistan. ISIL refers to Iran, Afghanistan, Pakistan, India, Tibet, Sri Lanka, Tajikistan, Uzbekistan, Kazakhstan, Kyrgyzstan, and Turkmenistan as "Wilayat Khorasan" or Korasan State. An ISIL affiliate, known as the Khorasan Group, has been fighting in Syria and is believed to be made up of central Asian ISIL recruits and commanders.

It was recently announced that Colonel Gulmurod Khalimov, the one-time head of the Tajikistan elite anti-terrorism police force, known as OMON, defected to ISIL and is now one its top field commanders in Syria. Khalimov, who was trained by U.S. Special Operations, Blackwater, and CIA officers during a number of official visits to the United States, has vowed to return to the Tajikistan to "slaughter" Tajik President Emomali Rakhmonov, recruit Tajiks working in Russia to launch terrorist attacks inside Russia itself and Tajiks in Tajikistan to attack Russian military troops stationed in Tajikistan (which makes Khalimov an ally of NATO top military commander General Philip Breedlove and U.S. Defense Secretary Ashton Carter, who want to increase military pressure on Russia to Cold War levels). ISIL guerrillas, mostly Chechens, fresh from combat in Syria and Iraq, have been discovered fighting for Ihor Kolomoisky's Israeli- and neo-Nazi-led mercenary battalions against the pro-Russian forces of Donetsk and Lugansk in Eastern Ukraine.

ISIL has, conveniently for the West, attacked Taliban forces in Afghanistan. The Taliban declared ISIL's self-declared caliphate as illegitimate, and its caliph leader, Abu Bakr al-Baghdadi, who may be an artificial product of the CIA's and Mossad's psychological warfare units, to be a fraud. The Taliban became alarmed as some of its members broke ranks with the jihadist movement and joined ISIL in Afghanistan and Pakistan. Moreover, ISIL declared the Taliban to be "kafirs", or unbelievers of Islam. In April, Al-Baghadi declared the Taliban's Mullah Omar to be "a fool and illiterate warlord." It is no coincidence that ISIL's rhetoric about the enigmatic Taliban leader matches nicely with that issued forth by the U.S. military psy-ops units in Afghanistan at the height of the U.S. military intervention in that country. In mid-June, ISIL released a video tape showing its forces decapitating a Taliban prisoner in Afghanistan.

ISIL has, also, in concert with increasing U.S. military pressure on China and North Korea, declared jihad or holy war on the two Asian nations. In May, a North Korean couple, who worked as doctors at the local hospital in Zallah, Libya, were taken captive by ISIL in Libya. No word has been received on the fate of the North Korean husband and wife medical duo. In January, ISIL computer hackers, known as the "Cyber Caliphate", claimed credit for altering the Facebook page of Air Koryo, North Korea's state-owned airline. ISIL's black and white flag was pasted on the Facebook page with a statement calling North Korea's leader Kim Jong Un "a crying pig." The ISIL hackers also had a warning for both North Korea and China: "North Korea, the communist thug nation, and the Chinese communist thugs will pay a price for their collaboration with the enemies of the mujahideen".

ISIL propaganda rhetoric about China and North Korea also coincide with pronouncements emanating from the U.S. Pacific Command in Hawaii about the military threats posed by Beijing and Pyongyang. North Korea has responded to the ISIL threats by providing the Type 73 machine gun, manufactured by the First Machine Industry Bureau of North Korea to Iraqi government and Kurdish forces fighting against ISIL in Iraq. North Korean military advisers are also believed to be assisting Syrian government and Lebanese Hezbollah forces battling ISIL in Syria. South Korea, which never misses an opportunity to confront North Korea militarily, permitted a South Korean citizen, known only by the very common Korean name "Kim", to join ISIL ranks in Syria in February. It is more likely that "Kim" is a South Korean intelligence agent who is responsible for coordinating ISIL attacks on North Korean assets in the region, including the North Korean medical couple in Libya.

Venezuela's president Nicolas Maduro, who the CIA is busy trying to overthrow, called ISIL a "Frankenstein, a monster nursed by the West itself" in a speech to the United Nations General Assembly in 2014. Not coincidentally, as President Barack Obama declared that Venezuela posed a "national security threat" to the United States in March, there were reports of nascent ISIL activity in Venezuela. The U.S. Army War College, including Professor Robert Bunker, began issuing statements that increased ISIL activity in Venezuela would be good for U.S. national security because ISIL is the natural enemy of Hezbollah, which the U.S. neocons are claiming has gained a strategic toehold in Venezuela. The links between ISIL and the West in Latin America have not been lost on the Western Hemisphere's sage senior statesman, former Cuban president Fidel Castro.

In September 2014, Castro accused Israel's Mossad, in league with Senator McCain, of helping to create ISIL.

The ultimate perpetrators of ISIL's ravaging of the Middle East are not to be found in the deserts of the Middle East and the mountains of Afghanistan but in the seventh floor director's suite at CIA headquarters in Langley. In 1985, the same year the CIA sponsored the summit of right-wing terrorist groups in Jamba, Angola, the CIA tried to kill Lebanon's Shi'a Grand Ayatollah Muhammad Hussein Fadl-Allah with a car bomb in Beirut. The CIA missed the ayatollah but killed 80 innocent people and wounded 256. Today, the CIA allows ISIL to get its fingers dirty in carrying out such terrorist attacks from Iraq and Syria to Yemen and Libya. ISIL cannot be brought to its knees without dealing harshly with Mr. Brennan and his top advisers.

Russia's Offer of Anti-ISIL Alliance Met with Obama Bluster

October 1, 2015. In his speech before the United Nations General Assembly, Russian President Vladimir Putin offered a proposal to create a coalition of nations to battle the Islamic State of Iraq and the Levant (ISIL). Putin's coalition would be modeled after the anti-Hitler coalition created by the Allies during World War II. But rather than magnanimously accept Russia's offer as did President Franklin Roosevelt in accepting Moscow's offer of an alliance against Nazi Germany in World War II, President Barack Obama resorted to his familiar grandstanding and bluster before the cameras and the assembled delegates in the General Assembly hall.

There would be no ISIL had it not been for Obama's foolhardy and dangerous game of deciding to stage "social network-based" revolutions in Libya, Syria, and other countries in furtherance of the idiotic "Responsibility to Protect" (R2P) casus belli engineered by two of the people who sat in the U.S. delegation as Obama spoke to the General Assembly. They were his former ambassador to the UN and now national security adviser Susan Rice, and his current ambassador to the UN Samantha Power. Both women are graduates of the George Soros school of fomenting international crises in furtherance of hedge fund profits on a grand scale.

The day after Putin's offer of an international grand coalition to take on ISIL, Obama offered up some weak-kneed measures, including imposing sanctions and asset freezes on 35 individuals and groups known for quite some time to have been supporters of ISIL. In addition, Obama said the U.S. was increasing its propaganda operations to deter "young people" from flocking to ISIL's ranks. Obama tried to steal the thunder from Putin's initiative by staging an "anti-terrorism summit" at the UN. Obama managed to invite a couple of U.S. "sock puppets", including Iraqi Prime Minister Haider al-Abadi, Nigerian President Muhammadu Buhari, and Norwegian Prime Minister Emma Solberg to his summit in order to give it the imprimatur of a global event.

For Obama and French Foreign Minister Laurent Fabius, the only way to defeat ISIL is to force Syrian President Bashar al-Assad from office. This insane policy is exactly how ISIL managed to gain control over a majority of Syrian territory and expand its control of land deep into Iraq. Obama fails to understand that it was the overthrow by NATO and the CIA of secular Arab leaders like Libya's Muammar Qaddafi and the attempt to overthrow the secular Assad that caused ISIL to gain so much power. Russia correctly understood Obama's policy of arming and training Syrian "moderates" was a joke, because, as General Lloyd Austin, the commander of the U.S. Central Command, stated in testimony before the U.S. Senate, the United States was only able to find "4 to 5" Syrian "moderates" to train as part of the phantom "Free Syrian Army." The Pentagon also confirmed that arms and ammunition provided to the phony Free Syrian Army made their way into the hands of the Al Nusra Front, allies of both Al Qaeda and ISIL, depending on the area of Syria involved and the day of the week.

It was the much-heralded late U.S. envoy to the Libyan Islamist rebels, Christopher Stevens, who set up a "rat line" of arms smuggling channels to the Syrian Islamists from arms caches captured from Qaddafi, who bears some of the blame for the specter of ISIL in Syria. It was a Central Intelligence Agency arms deal gone bad that resulted in Stevens' murder by Libyan arms smuggling rebels on September 12, 2012, at a CIA warehouse in Benghazi. This served as the impetus for the "Benghazi Gate" scandal that has tarnished then-Secretary of State Hillary Clinton, then-CIA director David Petraeus, and then-UN ambassador Susan Rice.

The CIA has always supported the most radical elements of Islamist guerrilla groups it incubates. The CIA always claims that it only supports Islamist groups committed to "democracy" and "moderation", but this is and always has been a flagrant lie.

At the very outset of the clandestine CIA support for the Afghan Mujaheddin against the socialist government of Afghanistan and its Soviet allies in 1979, the CIA always favored the most radical elements, because that is how America's allies in Saudi Arabia and Pakistan wanted it. The CIA gave military support to the most radical Mujaheddin warlord, Gulbudin Hekmatyar, leader of the Hezb-e Islami terrorist organization and prime minister of Afghanistan from 1993 to 1994. Today, Hekmatyar is allied with the Taliban against the Kabul government and U.S. forces.

When the Taliban began making gains in northern Afghanistan, ISIL, the Taliban's major enemy in Afghanistan, suspiciously began making gains in the eastern part of the country. This pattern has been seen in Syria and Iraq. As Syrian Kurds, who are neutral on Assad remaining in power, made gains in the northeast part of Syria, ISIL went on the offensive against the Kurds with the support of Turkey and its NATO benefactor, the United States. Similarly, as Iraqi Kurds, with the support of the forces of Kurdish forces in Turkey, consolidated their gains against ISIL in Iraq, ISIL, with the support of the Americans, Saudis, and Turks went on the offensive against the Kurds there. ISIL also approached the outer suburbs of Baghdad.

Obama wrongly believes ISIL's power is supplemented by a few hundred teenagers arriving from the West and other countries to join its ranks. If Obama ever showed leadership and sat John O. Brennan, his Wahhabist-oriented and pro-Saudi CIA director, down for a serious talk, Obama would realize that ISIL's support comes from decisions made inside the secure rooms of Langley, Virginia with the connivance of the intelligence services of Saudi Arabia, Turkey, Qatar, France, Britain, and Israel.

There is little doubt that the U.S. military and CIA have assisted ISIL forces on the ground in Syria, Iraq, and Afghanistan. U.S. and Israeli arms transfers to ISIL affiliated groups in Syria were identified by Iraqi officials in Baghdad and Kurdish officials in the regional capital of Erbil, who witnessed U.S. air drops of weapons and supplies to ISIL units in Anbar province in western Iraq and Iraqi Kurdistan. Israeli commandos were also seen handing off weapons to ISIL units operating in Anbar. ISIL-linked units received U.S. arms when members of an entity called the "New Syrian Forces" handed them over to the Nusra Front.

ISIL forces received training from U.S. Special Forces and the intelligence agencies of U.S. allies before they joined the terrorist group. These ISIL commanders include:

• Colonel Gulmurod Khalimov, the U.S. Special Forces-trained former commander of the Tajikistan OMON special forces.

• Georgian army veteran Tarkhan Batirashvili, also known as Abu Omar al Shishani, who was trained in special operations by the U.S. in Georgia.

• Ibrahim Samarrai, aka "Abu Bakr al-Baghdad", also known as the caliph of the Islamic State, is said by Iranian intelligence to have been an asset of the CIA.

• David Drugeon, former French DGSE intelligence officer, is a leader of the ISIL-allied Khorasan Group in Syria.

• Boubaker El-Hakim, a Tunisian terrorist linked to ISIL, was reportedly a French intelligence asset.

• Samantha Lewthwaite, also known as Sherafiyah Lewthwaite and the "White Widow", daughter of a British Army officer and graduate of the MI6-linked School of Oriental and African Studies in London, oversaw

Somali Al Shabaab attacks in Kenya. Al Shabaab has sworn allegiance to ISIL.

Many more Syrian rebels receiving training at a secret camp near Safawi, Jordan, have gone on to join ISIL ranks in Syria and Iraq.

Obama claims that ISIL has expanded due to the lack of opportunities for Muslim youth and a barrage of radical propaganda from Islamist extremist figures. He forgot to add another important reason for ISIL's rapid growth: the active support ISIL has received from the CIA, the Department of Defense, and U.S. allies in Turkey, Saudi Arabia, Israel, Qatar, United Arab Emirates, Britain, and France.

President Putin made an honest offer of a grand coalition to fight against ISIL. However, to date, the only parties to such a coalition that will take firm action against the Western-incubated terrorist group are Russia, Iran, the Syrian government of Bashar al Assad, Lebanese Hezbollah, China, and Iraq. With ISIL activity, especially the looting of artifacts for sale to unscrupulous Israeli black marketers, already being reported in the Gorno-Badakshan Autonomous Region of Tajikistan and Afghanistan's Badakshan province, perhaps Tajikistan and Afghanistan, including the Taliban, can be brought into the grand coalition. Other countries have a stark choice: either stick with Obama and his friends and see ISIL gain even more strength and territory, or opt for the Russo-Sino-Iranian coalition and see ISIL finally vanquished.

Welcome to "Erdoganstan": Bosna Hersek to Mongolistan

November 2, 2015 When Turkish President Recep Tayyip Erdogan's Justice and Development Party (AKP) first gained power in the parliamentary election of 2002, commentators foresaw a Turkey that would, while stressing some Islamist principles, remain a secular nation that would not interfere in the affairs of its closest neighbors and distant countries.

It was not long before the secularist Republican People's Party (CHP) that championed the non-Islamist guidance of Turkey's founder, Kemal Ataturk, were able to point to the pan-Islamist and pan-Turkic policies of then-Prime Minister Erdogan's government and say to those who originally bought into the AKP propaganda, "We told you so!"

There is a reason why Erdogan built for himself a palatial presidential palace in Ankara that evokes memories of the Seljuk Empire. Erdogan, who castigated the Ataturk hero-worship policies of the opposition CHP, has created his own cult of personality, one that advances a political philosophy that combines Islamist beliefs and Ottoman hegemony with Turanism.

When the AKP first came to power in Turkey, its government stated that Turkey would establish close relations with all nations, near and far. What it did not say was that this new international policy was aimed at forging close relations with the Wahhabist regimes of Saudi Arabia and the Gulf to depose secularist Arab socialist-based governments in Syria, Libya, Egypt, and Tunisia. Soon, Turkish arms were flowing to Islamist rebel groups composed of both pro-Saudi Salafists and pro-Qatari Muslim Brotherhood members in Syria and Libya. Both nations experienced "Arab Spring" revolutions egged on by George Soros's social media operatives under the umbrella of the Open Society Institute and the National Endowment for Democracy (NED).

Erdogan's envoys were also working closely with the Ennahda Movement in Tunisia and the Freedom and Justice Party of Egypt, both of which took their inspiration from the AKP and the Muslim Brotherhood. After Turkey's political offspring, Presidents Moncef Marzouki and Mohamed Morsi, took power in Tunisia and Egypt, they announced their support for the Islamist rebels in the Libyan and Syrian civil wars. Behind the scenes was Erdogan, whom President Barack Obama praised as a Muslim leader the United States relied on for its "outreach" to the Muslim world.

However, Erdogan's new international "outreach" is not limited to his Arab south. Advancing the pan-Turanian concept, which includes pan-Turkic notions with the idea that the Uralo-Altaic peoples constitute a distinct "Turanid" race, Erdogan has set course to include peoples stretching from Bosnia-Herzegovina (Bosna Hersek) in the Balkans to Japan in the Far East in a Turanian "commonwealth" of nations. Not only has Erdogan sat idly by while hundreds of thousands of Syrian, Iraqi, and Afghan migrants transited through Turkey to overwhelm Europe in a virtual Muslim invasion not seen since the Ottoman siege of Vienna of 1529, but his intelligence service, the "Millî İstihbarat Teşkilatı", or MIT, has facilitated the recruitment into the ranks of the Islamic State of Iraq and the Levant (ISIL), the Nusra Front, Al Qaeda, and the Khorasan Group of Muslim mercenaries from the claimed pan-Turanian lands of Chechnya (called Chechenistan by the Turks), Uzbekistan, Tajikistan, western China ("East Turkestan"), and Afghanistan.

Opposing these mercenaries are those who would suffer the most under Erdogan's concept of a new Ottoman-Seljuk Empire that would treat Muslim and Christian Kurds, Alawites, Shi'as, Armenians, Greeks, Maronite Christians, Russians, Ukrainians, Chinese, and others not recognized as full equals in an Ottoman-Seljuk Sunni Muslim/Turanian empire as second-class citizens and infidels.

In the minds of the pan-Turanians, any race not descended from the ancient Turks, who were led out of the Ergenekon Valley of Mongolia by "Asena," the "mother grey wolf" to whom all Turanids owe their existence, are not equal to the racially superior "grey wolf" peoples. The youth movements of many pan-Turanian political parties, including the Turkish Nationalist

Movement Party (MHP) and the Bozkurt Movement of Azerbaijan, use the "grey wolf" as their symbol. The inherent racial superiority notions of the pan-Turanians was noted with interest by Adolf Hitler's historians, and was a major reason for Nazi Germany to attempt to make common cause with Turkey under Ataturk.

When the array of nations being threatened by pan-Turanism is examined closely, it is clear that Erdogan has secretly made common cause with the enemies of Russia, that is, the Uralo-Altaic countries of Finland, Estonia, Latvia, Lithuania, as well as pro-Western elements in Hungary. The pan-Turanians claim Finns, Balts, Bulgars, and Magyars are members of the Turanid race, and this has not been lost on the NATO planners who have threatened Russia over its reclamation of Crimea and assistance to the Syrian Arab Republic. Crimea is not only claimed by Ukraine, which never had possession of the peninsula until 1954 when it was "gifted" to the Ukrainian Soviet Socialist Republic by Soviet Communist Party general secretary Nikita Khrushchev, but also by the Tatars, who are claimed by the pan-Turanian Turks to be the separate nation of "Tataristan".

In 2011, Erdogan visited Tatarstan, where President Rustam Minnikhanov hosted a lavish banquet for the then-prime minister of Turkey in Kazan, the Tatar capital. Tatarstan is not the only Turkic Muslim autonomous republic in Russia that Turkey is eyeing for increased influence. Turkish Airlines has inaugurated direct service between Istanbul and Ufa, the capital of Bashkortostan. The U.S. Central Intelligence Agency has taken advantage of a Chechen diaspora in Turkey to recruit agents for destabilization operations in the Russian Caucasus, as well as in Syria and Iraq. The accused co-bomber of the Boston Marathon, Tamerlan Tsarnaev, received special training in destabilization operations from CIA-supported and Turkey-based Chechens in Tbilisi and the Pankisi Gorge in Georgia.

There are also pan-Turanian movements in Japan that maintain affiliations with their counterparts in far-off Finland. There is little question that the Muslim Uighurs of western China are being assisted by not only the Turks but by the Soros-influenced resources of Radio Free Asia and the NED. The pan-Turanians not only see the Uighurs as part of their empire, but also the neighboring Mongols, whose homeland the Turks call "Mongolistan," and Manchus and Koreans.

Thanks to Erdogan's dream of a modern Ottoman-Seljuk pan-Turanian empire, we see military plans currently afoot by NATO to press Russia in the Baltic, Black Sea, Caucasus, and Mediterranean regions, and by Japan and its Pacific Rim allies of the United States, Australia, and New Zealand to box in China in the South China and East China Seas.

Japan's militaristic and revanchist prime minister Shinzo Abe has made common cause with his pan-Turanian ally Erdogan. During a recent visit to

Japan, Abe gave Japan's full support to Turkey in the current Syrian crisis. In other words, pan-Turanian nationalist Abe approves of the fact that Turkey is facilitating a Muslim invasion of Europe. What was the occasion of Erdogan's visit to Japan? It was classic pan-Turanism in action: Erdogan and Abe jointly marked the 125th anniversary of the sinking in 1890 of the Ottoman warship "Ertugrul" off of Wakayama prefecture in Japan. Although 500 Ottoman sailors died, 69 survived due to the efforts of the local Japanese villagers. Recognizing the sinking of the "Ertugrul" was Abe's way of tipping his hat to Erdogan's neo-Ottoman goals.

Erdogan's political opponents in Turkey have claimed he is "unbalanced". Regardless of his mental fitness, Erdogan sees the Eurasian map as comprising a Turanian commonwealth composed of Turkic and Turanian vassals and partners -- Abhazya, Acaristan, Adigey, Afganistan, Altay, Arnavutluk (Albania), Azerbaycan, Badakhshan, Başkurdistan, Bosna Hersek, Bulgaristan, Çeçenistan, Çuvaş, Ermenistan (Armenia), Estonya, Finlandiya, Gagavuzya (Gagauzia), Gürcistan (Georgia), Hakasya (Khakassia), İnguşya, Japoniya, Kalimikya, Karakalpakistan, Kazakistan, Kirgizistan, Kirim (Crimea), Komi, Kosova, Kuzey Kıbrıs Türk Cumhuriyeti (Turkish Republic of Northern Cyprus), Kore (Korea – North and South), Letonya (Latvia), Letuva (Lithuania), Macaristan (Hungary), Makedonya, Mançurya, Mari-El, Mizrah Türkestan (East Turkestan), Mongolistan, Özbekistan, Pakistan, Saha (Yakutia), Sirion (Syria), Tacikistan, Tataristan, Türkiye, Türkmenistan, Tüşluk Acerbaycan (South Azerbaijan – Iran), Tüşluk Osetya, Tuva, and Udmurtya.

Enter a number of offices and conference rooms controlled by Erdogan's AKP and one will notice most of the flags of these pan-Turanian nations and regions on full display. They represent Erdogan's dream of a pan-Turanian / Ottoman "Erdoganstan".

J'accuse: Those Responsible for the Friday the 13th Attacks in Paris

November 19, 2015 Almost immediately after the Friday the 13th terrorist attacks in Paris by the Islamic State of Iraq and the Levant (ISIL), that left 129 dead and 352 wounded - 100 severely - the chief enablers of the massive influx of Middle Eastern and North African migrants into Europe, which included jihadist "sleeper agents", proclaimed that casting blame for the attacks was outrageous at a time when people needed to mourn. The social media and propaganda operatives who are financed by George Soros's global network of non-governmental organization (NGO) fronts were squarely behind the campaign to encourage mainly Syrian migrants in Turkey to storm into Europe from refugee centers in Turkey.

The Soros gang's griping about casting blame on any migrants for the terrorist attacks was a cynical attempt to divert attention away from the fact that it was the Soros groups that enabled the terrorists to enter Europe by embedding themselves as Trojan horses inside the migrant stream. At a recent meeting in Istanbul, Soros called for the spending of 10 billion euros to facilitate the movement of more than a million Third World and mainly Muslim refugees into Europe.

While most refugees, particularly women and children who want to enter Europe are legitimate political and economic migrants, responding to German Chancellor Angela Merkel's blanket invitation, the Soros organization has cynically used the migrant issue to advance its own agenda.

Integrated in the mass of humanity that swamped the Balkans refugee bridgehead were ISIL terrorists who were intent on carrying out exactly the type of terrorist attacks witnessed in Paris. However, in a display of sheer audacity and using their well-honed polarization skills and "divide-and-conquer" techniques, the Soros operatives said that anyone casting blame on the migrants were racists and xenophobes. In response, it is important to state that Soros and his operatives directly enabled the creation of Europe's worst refugee crisis since the end of World War II are nothing more than aiders and abettors of jihadist terrorism. With their irresponsible methods of swamping Europe with uncontrollable streams of migrants, thus breaking down European security mechanisms, the Soros operatives have the blood of the innocent victims of ISIL's attacks on their own duplicitous hands.

Even after French authorities determined that one of the dead terrorists in Paris was, in fact, Ahmad Almohammad, a Syrian refugee from Idlib who entered Europe from Turkey on October 3 through the Greek isle of Leros with a Syrian passport, Soros's operatives demanded that the refugee flow from the Middle East, Asia, and North Africa continue unabated, despite the collapse of the Europe's external borders and regional security. Almohammad transited from Greece to Macedonia, Serbia, Croatia, Hungary, Austria, and then into Germany and, ultimately, to France. One such call to maintain the current migratory status quo came from the Emergencies Director of Human Rights Watch, Peter Bouckaert. It should be emphasized that in 2010 Soros "leased" Human Rights Watch for $100 million over a ten-year period. Since that time, the NGO has served Soros's sordid global interests, including undermining the government of Syrian president Bashar al-Assad and concocting phony news reports about "barrel bombs" and chemical weapons attacks by Syria's army. Bouckaert claimed the Syrian passport found on the dead terrorist migrant was fake. The claim turned out to be false.

Because of pressure from groups like Human Rights Watch, Amnesty International, International Organization of Migration, and other Soros-financed geopolitical tools, the Syrian government relaxed its stringent passport renewal policies, after it was criticized for doing nothing to help Syrians who had fled the civil war ravaging the country. In April 2015, Syrians abroad, even those who left the country illegally, members of exiled opposition groups, and Syrians who dodged the military draft, were permitted to renew their Syrian passports at Syrian consulates in Turkey, Greece, Lebanon, and the United Arab Emirates. This was a direct concession by Assad to the Syrian opposition before peace talks were due to commence in Geneva.

It was in Greece where the Friday the 13th Paris terrorist was issued his emergency Syrian passport, which Human Rights Watch misrepresented as counterfeit. Is Human Rights Watch perhaps trying to divert attention away from the fact that terrorists are obtaining valid passports to enter Europe?

Two other Soros-financed groups that have facilitated the entry of jihadist refugees into Europe are W2EU (Welcome to European Union) and MigrationAid Hungary. W2EU has provided migrants with "Rough Guide" booklets written in Arabic that instruct migrants, now known to have included terrorists, on how to travel to Germany and Austria and ask for asylum, food, housing, and unemployment benefits. It is clear that these Soros groups have worked hand-in-glove with Merkel, who shouted from her perch in Berlin for all refugees to come to Germany. Even when informed that there were jihadists among the refugee ranks, Merkel ordered that German borders remain open. She and her coalition government of Christian Democrats and Social Democrats also share in the blame for the Paris Friday the 13th massacre. Soros has also utilized NGOs such as the European Program for Integration and Migration (EPIM) to lobby for relaxed immigration controls by the European Union.

One minute after the first news reports of the Friday the 13th attacks, a London-based cartoonist named Jean Jullien claimed he designed the peace symbol with the Eiffel Tower image. The symbol became the trademark for memorializing the attack. Just as with the Charlie Hebdo attacks, slick marketing images were immediately rolled out. In the case of the Charlie Hebdo operation, new signs proclaiming "Je suis Charlie" appeared all over Paris and on social media within minutes. In the latest attack, the Eiffel Tower peace symbol went viral on social media and signs proclaiming "Je suis Paris" not only spread on the Internet but began popping up throughout France almost immediately. As seen with the themed revolution campaigns designed by Soros propaganda "majordomo" Gene Sharp, slick media production of emotion-laden symbols and slogans have become integral to Soros-linked social upheaval campaigns.

Also culpable is U.S. Assistant Secretary of State for European Affairs Victoria Nuland, the neoconservative tool of Benjamin Netanyahu and the

Israel Lobby, who presided over savaging Greece with a series of destabilizing economic austerity measures. As part of the team, Nuland undermined the government of Macedonia with a Ukrainian-style "color revolution" attempt. It was through Greece and Macedonia that the refugee invasion of Europe was launched. Neither country was in a position to defend its maritime and land frontiers.

As also seen with the Charlie Hebdo terrorist attacks in Paris, Netanyahu's Zionist power elites are again eager to make political capital out of any jihadist operation. Direct Israeli military and intelligence support for Syrian and Iraqi jihadist groups, including the Nusra Front and Al Qaeda, are common denominators of the two major jihadist attacks in Paris in 2015.

Just a day before the Friday the 13th attack, Barack Obama stressed that ISIL needed no elimination but mere "containment" in Syria and Iraq, Clearly, Obama merely communicated the desires of his Central Intelligence Agency director John Brennan, who is long-rumored to be Wahhabist-oriented, and who may well be the actual "Jihadi John". Incidentally, the U.S. claimed to have killed the video-documented "Jihadi John" just the day before the latest Paris attack. As usual which such blustering claims, as previously also seen with the "killing" of Osama bin Laden, the United States again failed to provide any solid proof that it killed the ISIL propagandist "Jihadi John".

Obama's and Brennan's coddling of ISIL through Washington's Saudi, Qatari, and Turkish proxies – Saudi King Salman, Qatar's Al Thani ruling clique, and Turkey's want-to-be Ottoman and Seljuk emperor Recep Tayyip Erdogan -- enabled the self-proclaimed Islamic "caliphate" to take hundreds of thousands of innocent lives in Syria, Iraq, the Kurdish region, Yemen, Libya, Nigeria, Sinai, Lebanon, Thailand, Bangladesh, Afghanistan, Tunisia, France, and Turkey. The hands of Erdogan, the House of Saud, and the House of Thani are dripping with the blood of the victims of ISIL.

Many Turks believe Erdogan used ISIL to carry out the deadly twin suicide bombings of Kurdish political demonstrations near Ankara's two train stations on October 10, 2015. Erdogan's increasingly draconian regime benefited from the pre-election bombing, as it enabled his party to gain a parliamentary majority. Erdogan blamed ISIL and the Kurdish PKK guerrilla group for the attack. Also noteworthy is the fact that two of the dead Friday the 13th terrorists in Paris were carrying altered Turkish passports.

At the November 15 G20 summit in the Turkish resort city of Antalya, Obama appeared to have taken a hiatus from seeking terrorism management advice from the ISIL-supporting Erdogan and, instead, was seen in private conference with Russian President Vladimir Putin to discuss battling the Islamic State. However, Obama's posturing was too little and too late. Any meaningful plan to combat jihadism in coordination with Russia, France, China, Iran, Egypt, and other countries would mandate the prerequisite of firing Brennan as CIA director and cleansing the intelligence agency of its Saudi- and Israeli-supporting elements.

The Islamic State is clearly not alone in having the blood of innocents on its hands. The trail of blood extends to Berlin, Riyadh, Doha, Ankara, as well as the White House and CIA headquarters in Langley, Virginia.

The Caribbean is America's "Balkans" for Jihadist Migrant Flow

November 25, 2015. Just as the Balkans have served as Europe's "soft underbelly" for the largest mass migration of refugees since World War II, the Caribbean, coupled with Central America, is proving to be America's own "Balkans" when it comes to Syrian and other migrants flowing into the United States. In the cases of both Europe and America, the flows of migrants, including non-vetted military draft-age men from Syria, Iraq, and other Muslim countries, is being facilitated by the huge network of non-governmental and quasi-governmental organizations influenced by and linked to the international hedge fund tycoon and all-around global troublemaker George Soros.

As revelations spread through the news media in Europe that among the refugees who streamed into Europe from Syria were some of the suicide bombers who launched the November 13 terrorist attacks in Paris, America was faced with reports that the Obama administration was preparing to accept at least 10,000 Syrian refugees. This resulted in calls for a moratorium from 31 state governors, including 30 Republicans and one Democrat, Maggie Hassan of New Hampshire; the governor of Guam; and former Ohio Democratic Governor Ted Strickland. Hassan and Strickland are candidates for the U.S. Senate in 2016. Many governors and other elected officials, including mayors and Republican and Democratic legislators, were unconvinced that the Obama administration, which has been under pressure from the Soros machine to lift all border restrictions, could or would adequately screen the migrants. The Obama administration insisted that vetting be conducted by the Department of Homeland Security, a department rife with incompetence, misbehavior by agents and officials, financial fraud, and bureaucratic turf battles.

As those who favor a moratorium on Syrian migrant placement in the United States came under vicious attack by irresponsible members of the "progressive" community, authorities in Honduras stopped five Syrian nationals who were trying to travel to the United States on fake Greek passports. These Syrians arrived from Costa Rica, the same country where Cubans, who are freely flying to countries in South America, are arriving in massive numbers in order to gain onward passage to the United States. Nicaragua has complained about a Cuban "invasion" of their nation, such as many Balkan nations have experienced with Middle Eastern migrants. For years, Soros has been trying to stir up Cubans against their government. With the advent of free travel abroad, the Soros operatives are now sponsoring Cuban emigration by air from the island. Destabilization of South and Central America has been the result of this migration. Now, with the addition of Syrian migrants to the mix, the same migratory routes used by the Cubans are now being employed by Syrians.

In July 2015, some 53 Syrians who arrived in the Caribbean nation of Antigua and Barbuda under a visa waiver program left by boat destined for the U.S. Virgin Islands. Nothing more was heard about what happened with the Syrians who entered U.S. territory seeking asylum due to religious persecution in Syria. The government of Antigua and Barbuda merely denied that it had sold the Syrians Antiguan passports under the Citizens by Investment Program (CIP). Antigua's opposition United Progressive Party warned that the Islamic State of Iraq and the Levant (ISIL) could take advantage of the CIP if Syrians, like Afghans, Iraqis, North Koreans, Somalis, Yemenis, and Iranians were not barred from participating in the "cash for passport" scheme.

The mysterious Syrian migrants in Antigua and their possible connection to jihadist terrorism was not the first time that Antigua figured prominently in terrorist activities. In 2004, two snipers, later said to be a homeless man and a teenage boy from Jamaica, shot at least 13 people in and around Washington, DC. Ten of them died. When Maryland police finally captured lead sniper John Allen Muhammad and his young companion, John Lee Malvo, the story began to grow international legs. At the time of his capture, it was learned that Muhammad was a former U.S. Army Sergeant who served in the Gulf War, and that he may have once been stationed with another U.S. Army Special Forces Sergeant named Ali Mohammed, who later became the chief training officer for Al Qaeda. It also was clear that Muhammad was far from homeless – he spent a lot of time in the Caribbean (where Ali Mohammed had recruited Al Qaeda members) and had been involved in a plot to kidnap Antigua's Prime Minister. Muhammad was apparently involved in a document forgery scheme on the island to illegally smuggle people, likely including jihadist terrorists, into the United States. Muhammad and Malvo possessed a Global Positioning System device and laptop computer, not the normal paraphernalia for homeless people.

In 2007, a Guyanese immigrant named Russell DeFreitas of Brooklyn was arrested in a plot, which the perpetrators called the "Chicken Farm" and "Chicken Hatchery," to blow up fuel storage tanks and pipelines at John F. Kennedy International Airport. DeFreitas, a cargo handler at JFK, had two Guyanese accomplices, Abdul Kadir, a former member of the Guyanese parliament, and Abdel Nur. In 2008, Kadir, Nur, and a Trinidadian, Kareem Ibrahim, were arrested in Trinidad and the three were extradited to the United States. The four terrorists were identified by the CIA as part of a jihadist cell operating in Guyana and Trinidad. One informant who ratted out the four terrorist plotters was a member of a violent cocaine and crack smuggling ring in Brooklyn. De Freitas and Kadir received life sentences.

In 2000, Guyanese immigrant Daron Wint, aka Darin Wint, Steffon Wint, and Dillion Wint, came at the age of 20 from Guyana to join his family in the United States. Wint sought to join the Marine Corps the next year. Wint, who attended Marine Corps Basic Training in Parris Island, South Carolina in September 2001, washed out for reasons the Marine Corps has not disclosed. In May 2015, Wint was charged with brutally torturing and murdering Greek-American businessman Savvas Savopoulos, his wife Amy, their 10-year old son Philip, and their El Salvadoran housekeeper Veralicia Figueroa at their $4.5 million home in northwest Washington, DC in the heart of Embassy Row. The murders took place after ISIL posted a video showing the White House with an ISIL flag flying over it. ISIL had threatened to attack Washington. The police never were open about others having been involved in the murder on Embassy Row. Washington police chief Cathy Lanier, in a news conference held outside the Savopoulos home after the discovery of their bodies, said the multiple homicide was "under investigation by the Joint Terrorism Task Force". Realizing her misstatement, Lanier quickly corrected herself, saying it was the "Joint Arson Task Force".

The Obama administration, which will go down in history as the most secretive on issues of national security, would never admit a jihadist threat from Caribbean waters. After the Paris attacks, St. Lucia decided to provide extra security for the French embassy in the capital of Castries, unusual for an idyllic island paradise. France extended its post-attack state of emergency to its Caribbean territories of Guadeloupe, French Guiana, Martinique, and St. Martin and St. Barthelemy.

Trinidad and Tobago's National Security Minister Edmund Dillon estimates that 80 Trinidad and Tobago citizens, including entire families, traveled to Syria to fight for ISIS. The Guyana government, concerned that Guyanese Muslims may be lured to fight for ISIL, are warning against any such temptation. In April 2015, a 16-year old Jamaican boy was deported from Suriname back to Jamaica after he was discovered to be heading to Syria, via the Netherlands and Turkey, to join ISIS. Paramaribo airport authorities disclosed the Jamaican was the third suspected ISIS recruit stopped before boarding a flight to Amsterdam.

An ISIL recruitment video released just prior to the Paris attacks showed three young Trinidadian children in the ISIL "capital" of Raqqa, Syria.

Obama criticized those who want to go slow on Syrian refugee immigration, proclaiming, quite petulantly, that the critics "are afraid of ... orphans".

The Obama administration now wants to convince the American people that they are safe from any Islamic State terrorists hiding among Syrian refugees. Many Americans are not buying Obama's reassurances, pabulum that is cooked up by Soros and his gang of media propagandists and crisis manipulators.

Only when Obama can assure, without any doubt, that the southern and eastern Caribbean maritime borders of the United States are safe – that no jihadists can gain entry into the United States from an arc extending from the Bahamas chain, south to the Windward and Leeward Islands, Hispaniola, Cuba, Jamaica, and South and Central America – should anyone believe the president.

Erdogan's Close Ties to ISIL

November 27, 2015. Turkish president Recep Tayyip Erdogan, contrary to the initial stated policies of his Justice and Development Party ("Adalet ve Kalkınma Partisi" or AKP), is not a moderate Muslim. Erdogan is slowly turning his nation into an Islamist revivalist entity mirroring the Ottoman Empire. In fact, Erdogan's personal amassing of wealth and his building of an opulent presidential palace in Ankara is also reminiscent of the old Seljuk Muslim emperors. Erdogan seems to relish in Turkey's imperialist past in every fashion imaginable.

Erdogan's newly-found wealth is courtesy of the Islamic State of Iraq and the Levant (ISIL), which has used Turkish middlemen to peddle their oil from Syria and Iraq to other countries through Turkey. One of these Turkish middlemen is reportedly Erdogan's son Necmettin Bilal Erdogan. The U.S. Treasury Department estimates that ISIL realizes $1 million a day from illicit oil sales on the world's petroleum spot market, with Erdogan's family cronies receiving a healthy portion of the ISIL oil proceeds.

The Turkish media has published photographs of the Harvard-educated Bilal Erdogan having dinner in an Istanbul restaurant with a notorious ISIL guerrilla leader who has been responsible for genocidal acts in Homs and Western Kurdistan in northeastern Syria. Bilal Erdogan is in the right business for illegally shipping oil on behalf of ISIL. He is one of three equal shareholders in "BMZ Group Denizcilik ve İnşaat Sanayi Anonim Şirketi", a marine shipping company.

There is little doubt that Erdogan has been using ISIL to battle his many enemies – all of whom stand opposed to Erdogan's Islamist and jihadist policies. Erdogan, through ISIL and its surrogates, including the Al Nusra Front and the Khorasan Group, has taken on Syria's secular government of

President Bashar al Assad; Kurdish groups in Turkey, Syria, and Iraq; Shi'as and Christian Armenians and Greeks in Lebanon; and the Shi'a government of Iraq. Erdogan has facilitated the crossing of ISIL commando units into Iran, and he continues to back Muslim Brotherhood factions in Egypt and Salafist brigades in Libya.

Erdogan who has also permitted the infiltration into Europe of ISIL terrorists, masquerading as refugees from Syria, yet he relies on the protection of NATO's mutual defense umbrella. With the military insurance policy provided by NATO, Erdogan has been emboldened to use ISIL and its affiliates as proxies for Turkey's greater aims: the establishment of a Turkish-dominated Islamist bloc from Morocco to western China – the goal of every Ottoman and Seljuk emperor.

One of the financial players involved in supporting Al Qaeda before the 9/11 attacks on the United States, Yasin al Qadi, a Saudi national, has been given unhindered free passage through Turkey by Erdogan. Between February and October 2012, al Qadi entered Turkey four times, even though he was subject to a United Nations Security Council travel ban. Turkish and Saudi pressure saw the UN remove al Qadi from the travel ban list after his fourth trip to Turkey in October 2012.

While Erdogan has publicly stated that he is a partner of the United States and NATO against ISIL, the facts on the ground speak for themselves. Erdogan's alleged military operations against ISIL have actually been a vicious campaign against the Kurdistan Workers' Party (PKK) in southeastern Turkey and the Syrian Kurdish PYD/YPG (Democratic Union Party) group in northeastern Syria. Erdogan has never had any desire to wage a war against ISIL. Instead, ISIL has committed egregious genocidal warfare against Kurds in Syria and Iraq.

The U.S. Congressional Research Service (CRS) has pointed out that Turkey is the favored route for ISIL terrorists to transfer to and from Syria. A CRS report, dated October 5, 2015, states: "Congress and other U.S. policymakers, along with many international actors, have shown significant concern about the use of Turkish territory by various groups and individuals involved in Syria's conflict—including foreign fighters from around the world—for transit, safe haven, and smuggling". The report quotes February 2015 congressional testimony from National Counterterrorism Center (NCTC) Director Nicholas Rasmussen: "Violent extremists take different routes, including land, air and sea. Most routes do involve transit through Turkey because of its geographic proximity to the Syrian border areas where most of these groups operate".

Rasmussen, in the same Congressional testimony, took aim at Erdogan's support for terrorists in Syria: "Turkey will always look at its interests through the prism of their own sense of self-interest, and how they prioritize particular requests that we make for cooperation doesn't always align with our prioritization". Turkey's "self-interest" is to promote jihadism and pan-Turkic Islamist ideology at the expense of the political stability of Syria, Iraq, Iran, Azerbaijan, Lebanon, Turkmenistan, Uzbekistan, Afghanistan, Kyrgyzstan, Kazakhstan, Tajikistan, Pakistan, Egypt, Libya, Tunisia, Sudan, Yemen, Algeria, Bosnia-Herzegovina, Kosovo, Macedonia, Bulgaria, and Morocco.

Turkey's Alevi minority, who are affiliated with the Syrian Alawites, have old links to Shi'a and Sufi Islam, and adhere to pre-Islamic Anatolian and Christian religious beliefs, have been called traitors to the Turkish state by Erdogan. The U.S. State Department summed up Erdogan's policies toward the Alevis in its Religious Freedom Report for 2013: "The government considers Alevism a heterodox Muslim sect and does not financially support religious worship for Alevi Muslims". The head of the secular Republican People's Party of Turkey (CHP), Kemal Kılıçdaroğlu, is an Alevi Muslim and he has supported the Assad government in Syria against its enemies. Erdogan has called Kılıçdaroğlu a traitor to Turkey.

Erdogan showed his commitment to ISIL terrorism when, after ISIL bombed a Russian Metrojet (Kogalymavia) Airbus enroute from Sharm el Sheikh to St. Petersburg, killing all 224 passengers and crew, he told Dubai TV, "The Russian airplanes are targeting Mujahidin in Syria and partisans fighting to topple Syrian dictator Assad. In Syria, Moscow seeks to tip the balance on the ground against 'our brethren.' Consequently, there should be no surprise if Islamic State take revenge". Erdogan added, "How can I condemn the Islamic State for shooting down a Russian plane as its passengers were returning from a happy vacation in a time when our co-religionists in Syria are bombed by Putin's fighter jets?.. it is the natural outcome of Moscow's actions in Syria and the support for Assad". Erdogan has even more reasons to support terrorist attacks on Egyptian soil. He continues to support the outlawed Muslim Brotherhood in Egypt and its imprisoned former Egyptian president, Mohamed Morsi. Russia supports Egypt's president Abdel Fattah al-Sisi.

In other words, less than a day after the terrorist murder of Russian citizens, including women and children, Erdogan could not wait to laud ISIL and its Sinai affiliate, "Ansar Bait al-Maqdis", for targeting Metrojet flight 9268, on October 31, 2015. More outrageously, the United States and NATO support the terrorism of Erdogan, which was once again displayed when Turkish-supported Syrian Turkoman guerrillas, operating under the NATO-supported "Free Syrian Army," shot at parachuting Russian Air Force Sukhoi-24 crewmen after their aircraft was shot out of the sky by Turkish F-16 interceptors.

These same jihadist Turkoman units fired a U.S.-supplied TOW missile at a Russian Marine search-and-rescue helicopter that came to save their downed pilots. One Russian pilot and a search-and-rescue Marine was killed in what constituted a Turkish-sanctioned violation of the Geneva Conventions on Warfare. It is Erdogan and his government that represent a true terrorist and jihadist state, and they seem intent on keeping up with the Saudis and Qataris in state-sponsored support for terrorism.

CIA-Islamic Jihadist Alliance Against Russia is 63 Years' Old

December 11, 2015. The dalliance of the U.S. Central Intelligence Agency with Islamic jihadist forces is nothing new. Today, the CIA provides weapons, training, and other support to jihadist-aligned domestic Syrian and foreign mercenary forces attempting to overthrow the government of the secular Syrian president, Bashar al Assad.

Among the recipients of CIA largesse are jihadist opposition forces in Syria that include Ahrar al-Sham, Jabhat al Nusra, Al Qaeda, the Khorasan Group, the Levant Front, Jabhat Ansar al-Islam, Brigade of Turkmen Mountain, Muslim Brotherhood of Syria, Ansar al-Sharia, Jabhat Ansar al-Din, Ghuraba al-Sham, Muhajirin wa-Ansar Alliance, Islamic Muthanna Movement, and the Imam Bukhari Jamaat. All of these groups have had alliances with or are part of the Islamic State of Iraq and the Levant (ISIL) and have sworn fealty to ISIL's elf-proclaimed caliphate. The last group on the list, Imam Bukhari Jammat, is an Uzbek jihadist mercenary group that helped ISIL capture parts of the Idlib region of Syria.

The use of Uzbek mercenaries by the CIA is almost as old as the American spy agency itself. In fact, CIA-Uzbek jihadist cooperation dates back some 63 years. According to its own formerly TOP SECRET Central Intelligence Bulletin, dated December 4, 1952, during the waning days of the Harry Truman administration, the CIA embarked on a program to foment nationalism tinged with jihadism among the Uzbek tribes of northern Afghanistan in order that it might spill across the border into the Uzbek Soviet Socialist Republic, a constituent republic of the Union of Soviet Socialist Republics.

This 1952 CIA policy of coopting Muslim radicals means that the current attempt by such anti-Russian U.S. official and quasi-official intelligence policy makers, including former Jimmy Carter national security adviser Zbigniew Brzezinski, hedge fund tycoon George Soros, and CIA director John Brennan, to bring about a radical Muslim destabilization of the Russian Federation is merely a continuation of past practice. Presently, this cabal of American Russophobes see a victory by jihadist forces in Syria, and ultimately in Iraq, will spill over into Russia's southern Caucasus region where jihadists have already been active, to central Asia.

In 1952, the CIA covertly incubated a band of Afghan Uzbeks. The Afghan Uzbek group, called the Mogul Band by the CIA, was reported by the CIA to have had "considerable strength in the northern part of the country" and "hoped to 'reunite' Afghan Uzbeks with fellow tribesmen across the Soviet frontier." The CIA also reported that the Afghan Uzbeks "tried to attract support" from mainly Shi'a Hazara tribal leaders in northern Afghanistan. However, the Sunni Uzbeks and the Shi'a Hazaras were unnatural allies, a fact that seems to have been lost on the CIA station operatives in Kabul assigned the task of radicalizing the Afghan Uzbeks into a potent anti-Soviet force.

The reference to the Mogul Band is the earliest example of the CIA using external Muslim forces against the Soviet Union. In the 1970s, the overthrow of the Afghan king and the establishment of a socialist republic in Afghanistan prompted the CIA to organize a jihadist army to fight against the secular Afghan government and its Soviet protectors. The jihadist army that fought the Soviets in Afghanistan was the CIA-fertilized embryo out of which the Taliban and Al Qaeda hatched. Al Qaeda eventually helped give birth to ISIL.

The CIA has not only used jihadists to target Soviet followed by Russian interests but also those of Serbs in Serbia, the Srpska Republic of Bosnia-Herzegovina, and Kosovo. The CIA-directed U.S. Agency for International Development (USAID) aided and abetted the rise of jihadism in the Balkans through the Balkans Transition Initiative and the Bosnian Transition Initiative. These would later serve as templates for similar operations in the majority Albanian but Serbian province of Kosovo that propelled the province to independence as a virtual U.S. and NATO colony and induced the demonization of the Serbian population in the northern part of Kosovo. The encouragement by the CIA and Soros's Open Society Institute NGO fronts in the region also led to the radicalization of Muslim population sectors of Bosnia-Herzegovina, the neighboring Muslim-majority Serbian region of Sandjak, remaining Muslim pockets in the Republic Srpska, and Albanian minority regions of Macedonia and Montenegro.

The same CIA-Soros cooperation can be seen today in the promotion of radical Wahhabist Islam in Syria, Iraq, Lebanon, Turkey, Libya, and other countries, especially operations involving the "Arab Spring" upheavals and their aftermath. The roots of this unholy alliance of the CIA, Soros, and Wahhabists has its roots in the media and propaganda operations in the former Yugoslavia and the Bill Clinton administration. First aimed at Serbia, these jihadist forces are now taking aim at Russia from their bases of operation in Syria, Iraq, and Turkey. Turkey, as well as fascist-dominated western and central Ukraine, have served as important bases of operations for anti-Russian jihadists from Chechnya, Ingushetia, Dagestan, and other Russian republics where Turkish- and Saudi-financed Islamist clerics have been stirring up trouble.

The CIA station chief in Kabul during the late 1970s was the grandfather of the modern Afghan jihadist mujaheddin, which begat Al Qaeda, which begat the Islamic State. Station chief John J. Reagan first met with Afghan mujaheddin leaders in Pakistan in May 1979 and promised them weapons and ammunition. However, President Carter did not authorize such transfers of weapons to the jihadists until July 1979, two months after John Reagan took it upon himself to forge an alliance with the Afghan mujaheddin fighting the Soviets in Afghanistan. The two months of unauthorized CIA help to the mujaheddin was arranged by Carter's national security adviser, Brzezinski, whose hatred for the Soviets and Russians had no bounds.

The CIA decided to import radical jihadists from the Middle East and North Africa into northwest Pakistan as mercenaries to assist the Afghan mujaheddin in their war against the Soviets. Much of the funding for this operation was "off-the-books" because it was provided by Saudi Arabia and certain wealthy Saudi families. One of their numbers, Osama Bin Laden, eventually arrived in northwest Pakistan to take up arms with the "Arab Afghans" fighting the Soviets and socialist and quite secular Afghan government in Kabul. To coordinate the arrival, training, and arming of the Arab Afghans was veteran CIA field agent Milton Bearden. In an interview with the BBC, Bearden said President Ronald Reagan's CIA director, William Casey, told him, "'I want you to go to Afghanistan, I want you to go next month and I will give you whatever you need to win'... He gave me the Stinger missiles and a billion dollars!"

Eventually, some of the Arab Afghans left Afghanistan and returned to their native Egypt, Saudi Arabia, Syria, Libya, Algeria, Tunisia, and Yemen and, with the exception of Saudi Arabia, they took up arms against their own governments. The Saudis paid off the mujaheddin veterans, including Osama Bin Laden, not to attack the "kingdom", preferring them to wage jihad in the name of the Wahhabi Islamic sect against the United States, Russia, Syria, Egypt, Morocco, and other countries. The Wahhabist jihadists also strictly avoided attacking Israel or Israeli interests.

Today, many of the veteran Arab Afghan jihadists are fighting as senior field commanders for the ISIL and Al Qaeda in Syria, Libya, and Yemen armed with weapons provided by the CIA, now under the directorship of the pro-Saudi / pro-Israeli CIA chief Brennan. Had President Truman nixed the CIA's dealings with jihadist members of the Mogul Gang in 1952, the Middle East and the Balkans might have become much different and more peaceful places.

The Brussels Bombings:

False Flag. or ISIS International?

False flag terror operations are part of a "strategy of tension," to galvanize public emotion against a chosen enemy, and distract people from the decline in the standard of living, as Adam Curtis so ably demonstrated in his film, *The Power of Nightmares.* 9/11 was arguably the most awesome false flag terror operation of all time. It inoculated society with a massive dose of "war on terror" and Islamophobia viruses, but frequent booster shots are still needed.

25

"People don't want to go to war anymore, so instead they are bringing the war to the people."

If you've been following black ops since 9/11, the pattern is monotonous by now: "Give Us This Day Our Daily False-Flag Gladio Op." One can understand Paul Craig Roberts when he writes,

---

[25] Image from http://www.sott.net/article/315080-Former-Israeli-Intel-Operatives-Run-Security-at-Brussels-Airport

I have not looked into the latest attack blamed on ISIS, this time in Belgium, and I am not going to investigate it. The explanation was set in stone by the initial reporting, and any skepticism that is expressed is disregarded as conspiracy theory.[26]

But let's investigate it anyway.

In the nearly 15 years since 9/11, the wispy fiction of Al Qaeda with the box cutters grew like the genie from the bottle into ISIS, a real existing military force. The mainstream media announce the bombings as "attacks claimed by Islamic State," conjuring the new bogeyman of an "Islamic" enemy "nation." A much more riveting target for war propaganda than that faceless meme, "the war on terror."

ISIS is so notorious for its savagery in Syria that a suicide bombing in Europe requires no great stretch of the imagination. Would the Muslim pariahs needed to quicken the drumbeat of the "war on terror" recruit themselves, as do-it-yourselfers? in this age of self-service via the internet, drenched with decades of Saudi financing of extremist Islam.

Things evolve. On 9/11 we were served up a litany of impossibilities: hijackers who were not on the passenger list, taking over jetliners armed only with small knives, to fly planes they could never have flown, at speeds those planes can't handle at low altitudes, to hit skyscrapers even a trained pilot could not have hit, and bring them straight down at free-fall speed, which can only be done by strategically placing powerful explosives, and is utterly impossible using airplanes or jet fuel. One impossibility upon another.

Whereas in Brussels, their narrative has elements of plausibility. ISIS apparently *has* used suicide bombers in Syria, for one thing. On the other hand, the sheer physical impossibility of the official 9/11 narrative serves as a benchmark for the *a priori* reliability of all the official terrorism narratives, which is between zero and minus infinity.

Since it's not my agenda to defend ISIS, does it matter whether ISIS really bombed Brussels in its war on Christendom? Especially since we argue here that ISIS is a creation of the Anglo-Zionist enemies of Islam, so ISIS is flying a false flag 24/7 no matter what. Yet oversimplification is not the friend of truth.

---

[26] http://www.paulcraigroberts.org/2016/03/25/is-the-latest-isis-attack-another-false-flag-paul-craig-roberts/

There is a good deal of evidence that the Friday the 13th or 11/13/15 massacre in Paris was a Gladio-style false flag.[27] The attackers were said to be from Belgium, from the same cell that carried out the Brussels bombings 130 days later, on 3/22/16.

Seen on its own, the Brussels attentat was also replete with markers of the classic patsy and controller paradigm of a black op propaganda event, which add up to a good case for a Gladio-style operation:

• **The attacks on the metro station.** Attacks on passenger rail stations are a traditional hallmark of the Gladio fascist falange. There was the deadly attack of August 1980 on Stazione Central in Bologna, a city famous as a communist party bastion. There were the March 11, 2004 Madrid train bombings, and the July 7, 2005 London Tube bombings.[28] The only difference now is the manufactured enemy and clash of civilizations is Islam rather than Communism, which has been labeled "Gladio B" by Sibel Edmonds.[29]

• **Innocent civilian victims,** when a serious adversary would single out military targets, which are so plentiful in Brussels. And why would ISIS hit Brussels, the seat of NATO, the force which gave them sway over Libya, which has provided them so much aid? Why do they not strike at Israel, or Russia, if the attacks are authentic, and not in fact an auto-goal scored by the local secret services?

• **Backhanded victim profiles.** Blowing up a carriage in the metro, one stop before the Islamic Center, would inflict more casualties on low-income, immigrant and Muslim victims. In Paris in November 2015, liberal-left leaning establishments were targeted, and many victims were Arabs attending a birthday party of a Tunisian girl there.

In the original Gladio 1978 case, why did the Red Brigades murder the Christian Democratic leader, Aldo Moro, who was the very figure working to allow the Italian Communist Party into a coalition government? JFK's enemies tried to blame his murder on Khrushchev, when in fact they themselves were behind it, and were not happy that Kennedy and Khrushchev had become friends.

As Kevin Barrett noted right after the Charlie Hebdo attacks,[30]

---

[27] *ISIS is US: The Shocking Truth Behind the Army of Terror.*

[28] *Terror on the Tube: Behind the Veil of 7/7, an Investigation,* by Nick Kollerstrom, Progressive Press, 3rd. ed,, 2012.

[29] https://wikispooks.com/wiki/Operation_Gladio

[30] http://www.veteranstoday.com/2015/01/08/charlie-hebdo-viral/

In 2011, Norway's Labor Party's youth wing was poised to impose a complete blockade on Israel. Suddenly the entire leadership of the Party's youth wing was slaughtered in a professional operation falsely attributed to a lone nut, Anders Breivik.[31]

In late 2013, Malaysia's Kuala Lumpur Tribunal found Israel guilty of genocide. A few months later, Malaysian planes started falling out of the sky.

Malaysia Airlines went into bankruptcy and barely survived.

• **Sting operations.** Human beings don't just become terrorists without being helped or pushed. According to Human Rights Watch,

> Nearly all of the highest-profile domestic terrorism plots in the United States since 9/11 featured the "direct involvement" of government agents or informants. In some cases the FBI may have created terrorists out of law-abiding individuals by suggesting the idea of taking terrorist action or encouraging the target to act."[32]

An HRW spokeswoman said, "many of these people would never have committed a crime if not for law enforcement encouraging, pressuring, and sometimes paying them to commit terrorist acts."[33]

[34]

---

[31] *Gladio, NATO's Dagger at the Heart of Europe*, p. 432-443.

[32] http://www.theguardian.com/world/2014/jul/21/government-agents-directly-involved-us-terror-plots-report

[33] https://www.hrw.org/news/2014/07/21/us-terrorism-prosecutions-often-illusion

[34] Image from "FBI Informant Exposes Sting Operation Targeting Innocent Americans in New "(T)ERROR" Documentary,"
http://www.democracynow.org/2015/4/20/fbi_informant_exposes_sting_operation_t
argeting

According to a New York Times op-ed on the story,

> Typically, the stings initially target suspects for pure speech — comments to an informer outside a mosque, angry postings on Web sites, e-mails with radicals overseas — then woo them into relationships with informers, who are often convicted felons working in exchange for leniency, or with F.B.I. agents posing as members of Al Qaeda or other groups...

> In one case, the FBI provided fake explosives, and drove the targeted individual to the site, where he "punched a number into a cellphone and got no boom, only a bust."[35]

The World Trade Center bombing of 1993 was exactly such a case, except the FBI switched real explosives for the fake stuff. The same thing might well have happened in Brussels.

• **Patsy profiles.** The typical terrorist patsy is a small-time criminal, often a drug addict of feeble intelligence. After a scrape with the police, there is a plea bargain leading to "undercover work" as an informer, in anti-terror drills, infiltrating "terrorist" cells, and so on. The victim may be too stupid, dazed or helpless to realize how suicidal this "gig" can get.

Here is one profile of the alleged mastermind of the Paris and Brussels bombings:[36]

> "We had him down as a rent boy, he was always hanging out with that kind of crowd," said Julien, a bartender at a gay club Salah Abdeslam visited..." His brother, Ibrahim, who blew himself up outside the Comptoire Voltaire Cafe, ran a bar in Brussels' now-infamous Molenbeek district. Their friend Karim told the Sunday Times that the bar was closed down a week before the attacks because Ibrahim had used it as a den to sell drugs. "[Ibrahim] and Salah spent most of their days smoking hashish and playing on Playstation in the bar," he said. Islamic State, who ordered the deadly attacks on the French capital, consider drug use and homosexuality sins, and routinely throws gay men to their deaths off of high buildings."

These guys are religious extremists bent on terrorism? dOES nOT cOMPUTE...

Remember Mohamed Atta and the alleged 19 9/11 hijackers who spent their time drinking, lap-dancing, and consorting with whores,

---

[35] http://www.nytimes.com/2012/04/29/opinion/sunday/terrorist-plots-helped-along-by-the-fbi.html

[36] http://www.breitbart.com/london/2015/11/23/paris-terrorist-gay-rent-boy-run-islamic-state-police/

paid for by the US taxpayer. They were completely oblivious of the Islamic religion.

One blog comment about Abdeslam pegged him as the kind of person who would do anything for money, which could be an apt guess.

The Bakraoui brothers, who allegedly blew up their luggage carts in Zaventem airport, had criminal records but were on probation.

"Brahim El Bakraoui was convicted in 2010 of shooting at police officers with a Kalashnikov during the process of committing an armed robbery... Khalid was convicted for a number of carjackings in 2011."[37] Reason enough to help the police with their enquiries.

• **The patsies usually don't survive** to tell the court their story -- most famous example: Lee Harvey Oswald.

It was reported that Abdeslam was originally only the driver for the gang. In Paris he allegedly survived because his suicide pack didn't explode. In Brussels he was saved by the bell again, arrested a couple days before the attacks. One conjecture is that his role might have been a handler or mole. The man in white seen with the Bakraouis pushing their trolleys in the airport "escaped," and could also be an intelligence service handler. (Such half-patsy, half-handler figures are also at high risk.)

Purported CCTV image of Ibrahim el-Bakraoui (centre) and Najim Laachraoui (left) in Zaventem Airport on the morning of 3/22. The third man is unidentified.

---

[37] http://www.activistpost.com/2016/03/signs-of-false-flag-in-brussels.html

Note that their luggage is on carts, not in body belts or backpacks. They didn't have to kill themselves; they could have detonated their suitcases with their cell phones, and escape in the confusion.

> A new kind of 'suicide bomber' emerges who pushes his bomb around on an airport trolley and dies as it explodes even though he could just walk off and live if he wanted to. Whether a bomb explodes accidentally, by remote control or if a "bomber" believes he has a shipment of cocaine in his bag, he's still most likely to be termed a "suicide bomber" in the news.[38]

One writer doubts this image is authentic because it was released too quickly.[39] Authentic or not, does it prove guilt, and what other evidence do we have that the bombs were set off by the accused? The Moroccan taxi driver who brought the bombers to the airport came forward, conveniently enough, but he also remains anonymous, conveniently enough, so this could be fiction, or perhaps part of the trap. In both the Paris attacks last year, some witnesses saw gunmen who looked more like Caucasian special forces than Muslim terrorists. In short, a police narrative is only as convincing as your trust in the police.

• **The theme of two brothers** comes up again with the Bakraoui brothers, with several recent precedents. The patsies in the Boston Marathon bombing were the Tsarnaev brothers. The Charlie Hebdo attacks of January 2015 in Paris starred the Kouachi brothers, who "were well known to police." Petty criminal Mohamed Merah of the Toulouse attacks and his brother were also on the police books. In the London bombings, the four patsies were not brothers, but close friends.

Brothers or close friends make useful targets because they are more likely to stay together and keep a secret. Patsies must never share the fact that they are doing undercover work for the police.

• **Iconic targets,** like the WTC and the Pentagon on 9/11. Brussels is the capital city of the European Union. There were also hints of a threat against a nuclear plant in Belgium. This is also a reminder of 9/11, when half a dozen suspects of "Middle Eastern appearance" were arrested in possession of plans for oil pipelines and nuclear

---

[38] http://www.911forum.org.uk/board/viewtopic.php?p=172224#172224
[39] http://www.globalresearch.ca/brussels-terror-attacks-masterminds-fake-cctv-footage-eu-funded-terror-drills-prior-knowledge/5516703

power plants. When they turned out to be Israelis, they were released without charges.[40]

• **Patsies must be protected** from prosecution up until they carry out their assignment. Thus the "Brussels safe house" remained safe for four months after the police learned that the gang was staying there.[41] Warnings went unheeded due to "bungling." While Salah Abdeslam was making his getaway from Paris back to Brussels, the car was stopped and let go by police three times.[42]

Israel's leading newspaper Ha'aretz reported,[43]

> Despite the advance warning, the intelligence and security preparedness in Brussels, where most of the European Union agencies are located, was limited in its scope and insufficient for the severity and immediacy of the alert.

> As far as is known, the attacks were planned by the headquarters of the Islamic State (ISIS) in Raqqa, Syria, which it has pronounced as the capital of its Islamic caliphate.

Nice plug there for ISIS and "our enemies are your enemies." With this announcement are the Israelis trying to get more security contracts in Brussels, or do they know all this because they already have the contracts?

Brussels underwent a total lockdown after the 11/13/15 Paris bombings, which only served the strategy of tension, rather than preventing attacks. Followed by relaxation, to catch people off guard. Timing is everything in building suspense and shock, and playing on emotions.

After 11/13/15, even Donald Trump warned that all was not well in Brussels, calling it a hell-hole where unassimilated immigrants are demanding sharia law.

An even more acute warning came from the Sultan of ISIS, caliph of Gladio and megalomaniac dictator of Turkey, the mad dog Tayyip Recep Erdogan, after the suicide bombings in Turkey (Ankara on Feb. 17 and March 13, Istanbul on March 19). These were the latest in a

---

[40] http://whatreallyhappened.com/WRHARTICLES/hundreds.html

[41] http://www.dailymail.co.uk/news/article-3509082/Bungling-Belgian-police-knew-Paris-bomber-Abdeslam-s-secret-hideout-THREE-MONTHS-did-planned-machine-gun-massacre-EASTER.html

[42] http://www.dailymail.co.uk/news/article-3367759/Police-stopped-Europe-s-wanted-terrorist-THREE-times-hours-immediately-Paris-attacks-released-time-according-getaway-driver.html

[43] http://www.haaretz.com/world-news/1.710572

series of attacks that have only benefited his dictatorship and damaged the interests of the moderate Kurdish minority, presumably arranged by the Turkish deep state Gray Wolves Gladio outfit Ergenekon, to blame on the Kurds and shore up the government. In a speech rebuking Brussels for hosting Kurdish protesters, the Mad Dog of NATO howled:

> There is no reason why the bomb that exploded in Ankara cannot explode in Brussels, in any other European city... The snakes you are sleeping with can bite you any time.[44]

There has been speculation that Erdogan gave ISIS the order to attack Brussels. It is interesting that the Bakraoui brothers had traveled briefly to Turkey. If they were in fact patsies in a false flag, then it's likely that Turkish intelligence would keep him in the loop, so the bombastic Erdogan was putting his foreknowledge to propagandistic effect. On 3/22, his state-run newspaper immediately blamed the Brussels bombing on the Kurds.[45] There is method in his madness. As the attack dog for NATO and Israel, he can get off his leash to savage the Kurds. Meanwhile his masters, the Anglo-Zionist empire, have his regime as a countergang to drive the Muslim world even madder than their Saudis running dogs already have.

Erdogan claims that Turkey deported Ibrahim al Bakraoui back to the Netherlands in summer 2015, under suspicion of being a "foreign fighter," and warned Belgium that he was a terrorist.[46] While this could have been normal police work, it is odd when Turkey is the transit expressway for tens of thousands of foreign jihadis joining ISIS in Syria. The idea could be to build a terrorist profile for the Brussels gang, while scoring a propaganda coup for Turkey, which is under heavy criticism for supporting ISIS.

What Bakraoui and companions were doing in Turkey is unknown but here is a plausible conjecture. Perhaps they were interested in the pay for joining ISIS in Syria, were picked up for questioning and were steered via Ergenekon, the Turkish Gladio, to take up work back in Brussels instead, whether "for ISIS" or for the police. An example could be carrying out drills to test the feasibility of suicide attacks. Given their criminal prowess, a suitable (but fake) job offer could be hit man. In a false flag, the hapless patsies take the blame, while special forces hit men carry out the deed. They are well-paid and well-protected. So the crooks fell into a trap that was way more crooked than they were.

• **Security stripping.** A strange link to major false flags of the 21st century is the firm that handles security operations for Brussels Zaventem Airport, the scene of the bombings. It's Israeli security firm ICTS, the oddly named "International Consultants on Targeted Security." Targeted indeed — turned on or off as needed, and quite a record it is.[47]

ICTS let the "Christmas underwear bomber" board a flight for Detroit at Amsterdam Schipol Airport in 2009 — without a passport, with no luggage and a one-way ticket.

ICTS let the "shoe bomber" patsy Richard Reid board flights for Tel Aviv and Miami from Paris Charles de Gaulle Airport.

ICTS had the security contracts for Boston Logan Airport, where flights allegedly took off with hijackers on board who steered them into the Twin Towers on 9/11; although their names were never on the passenger list.

ICTS was tightly linked to the 7/7/05 London Tube bombings.

> The main UK base for ICTS is in Luton [where the fatal four lads from Leeds boarded their train to London on 7/7/2005]... ICTS UK Ltd. has its office in Tavistock Square, right in front of the spot at which the 30 bus blew up [after it was diverted there by plainclothes police cars] ... in May 2005, ICTS International ... landed a contract for the London tube.[48]

The founder and chairman of ICTS is an Israeli gangster, Menachem J. Atzmon, high-ranking Likud figure and crime partner of one-time Israeli Prime Minister Ehud Olmert. Atzmon was convicted in Israel of election fraud, embezzlement, stealing from charities.

• **Numerology**

Another link to major false flags is cabbalistic numerology. The date of the bombings, 3/22, is said to be a major Satanic holiday invoking the goddess Isis![49] (It can also be the Iranian or Zoroastrian

---

[47] http://www.sott.net/article/315080-Former-Israeli-Intel-Operatives-Run-Security-at-Brussels-Airport

[48] *Terror on the Tube*, p. 284

[49] http://www.boilingfrogspost.com/2016/03/26/sean-stone-presents-brussels-attack-false-flag-theories-explored-with-sibel-edmonds-kevin-barrett/

New Year, or the first day of Spring.) 3/22 equals 322, the symbol of the Skull and Bones Club of Bush and Kerry fame. 22 = 2 x 11. Eleven is the number of destruction, of judgment and of Satan.[50] Eleven and thirteen are favorite Illuminati ciphers. The Paris attacks occurred on Friday, 11/13. The defeat of Germany was sealed on 11/11/18 at 11 a.m, which is also the exact start of the Fasching or Carnival season. JFK was murdered on 11/22/63, and 63=6+3=9, so this too was a date like 9/11.

The Brussels metro bombing was at 9:11 a.m. The airport bombings occurred just nine seconds apart at 11 minutes to 8, in different parts of the airport, suggesting remote detonation.

Chapter 13 in *Terror on the Tube* is entitled "Magic Numbers and Synchronous Detonations." The 9/11 attacks were on 9/11/01. Add one to each term of 9/11/01 and you get 10/12/02, the date of the Bali bomb. The Madrid train bombings were on 3/11/04, exactly 911 days after 9/11.

The London Tube Bombings were on 7/7/2005, which works out to 7/7/7 or 777. The tube blasts were closely synchronized: all four trains were hit at 11 minutes to 9 a.m.

A year later, on 7/11/06, there were the Mumbai bombings. Seven trains were bombed over a period of eleven minutes, on 11/7.

Many of these attacks involved the figure four: four planes on 9/11, four trains in Madrid, four trains and four patsies in London.

> There was also a series of four truck bombs in 2003 in Istanbul. The first two on Nov. 15th [the eleventh month] targeted synagogues and the second pair, on Nov. 20th, the HSBC bank and an empty British consulate. The second set of bombs went off at 9.10 and 9.12 GMT, that is, within one minute of 9.11 am British time, or 11.11 Turkish time.[51]

Here is what Kevin Barrett wrote on 3/22:[52]

> 3/22 false flag! Gladio strikes Brussels on satanic holiday
> "Radical Muslims" (meaning fanatical wahhabis and other extreme-puritanical types) do not celebrate other people's holidays...least of all the holidays of satanists...
> I've been a Muslim since 1993, and have a Ph.D. with an Islamic Studies component. One thing I can tell you is that observing satanic

---

[50] http://helpfreetheearth.com/news565_numbers.html
[51] *Terror on the Tube*, p. 188
[52] http://www.veteranstoday.com/2016/03/22/322/

holy dates associated with Isis and Ishtar is just not "Islamically kosher."

Muslims are not big on pagan goddesses. Trust me.

ISIS is a US-Zionist group. It has nothing to do with Islam.

Wahhabis are not big on the Illuminati or their numerology, either. (Arabic has its own much more sophisticated alphabetic-numeric code system, which fundamentalists probably detest for its mystical-literary allure and multiplying of meanings.)

It's the Western elite who dabble in the numbers game. One use for elevenish dates is to signal to initiates that it's "their" operation. The pseudo-mystical mumbo-jumbo could also help shield them from natural guilt feelings about their crimes.[53]

The numerology hocus pocus has gotten so obvious that one blogger predicted a false flag on 3/22/16:

> In a post titled "What's happening on March 22?" lordrothschild asked: "So, does anyone have any theories as to what the Illuminati will do on the 22nd of March this year? Will it be the date of the planned ISIS attack on Big Ben in London, where the tower is supposed to be blown up?"[54]

Reasonably good guess, but I don't think the Brits would stand for it. Unless ICTS gets the security contract.

• Wildly serendipitous or planted evidence. One of the Bakraoui brothers supposedly left a suicide note on a laptop which was found in a trashcan. Two alleged hijacker passports were miraculously found in the rubble of 9/11. In the Charlie Hebdo attacks, Kouachi's ID card was left in the getaway car. Lee Harvey Oswald dropped his wallet where it was sure to be found, and James Earl Ray, the framed killer of Martin Luther King, left a bundle on the sidewalk near the scene with "his rifle, binoculars, clothing, his prison radio, and a newspaper clipping revealing where King would be staying."[55] The court thanks you for the complete set of evidence.

Mohamed Atta of 9/11 fame was also a most prodigious example.

> Atta's luggage never made it on board on American Airlines' Boston Flight 11 even though there was almost an hour for the luggage to be loaded. It was used as "evidence" to prove that Arab "hijackers" took over the 9/11 planes. Found (rather "placed") in Atta's luggage was a

---

[53] *ISIS is US,* chapter on Paris 11/13/15

[54] http://www.vocativ.com/news/300355/false-flag-brussels/

[55] http://whowhatwhy.org/2015/02/01/lost-found-id-oddity-terror-cases-stupid-sinister/

copy of the Koran; an Islamic paradise wedding suit; a letter written by Atta that he planned to kill himself so that he could go to paradise as an Islamic martyr; and instructional videos for flying Boeing airliners.[56]

Atta was the only passenger whose bags didn't make it on the plane.

The London Tube scapegoats supposedly left explosives behind in their rental car.[57]

So was Brussels just another cookie-cutter false-flag operation?

A bit more artful than that. What's paradoxical about Brussels is that if the suspects were part of the same group as those killed carrying out the Paris attacks, they could hardly continue as dupes in a police set-up. So the alleged Ibrahim Bakraoui suicide note portrays the anxiety of a hunted man: "I am always on the move, I don't know what to do, I'm being hunted everywhere and am no longer safe. If I go on like this I will end up in a prison cell next to him." Supposedly it was accompanied by an audio message saying he would rather blow himself up than go to jail.[58]

Nail bombs and TATP (acetone peroxide) explosives were also y found in their apartment, if the police are to be believed. But since the feasibility of home-made TATP bombs has been fairly well debunked, this is rather a serious gaffe.[59] ISIS suicide bombers in Syria are on record as using C4 and explosive taken from artillery shells,[60] but the prosecutor in the Paris 11/13/15 attacks charged that the suspects used TATP in their suicide belts. TATP is favored for Gladio-type false flag narratives because it shores up the myth of home-brewed terror, requiring a yet stronger surveillance state. If terrorists used military explosives, rather than off-the-shelf ingredients, they might be traced to the source.

Were the suspects suicidal? There is no indication of religious fervor or terrorist leanings, no membership in any mosque, only a criminal past with these unfortunates. ISIS has been characterized as

---

[56] https://wideawakegentile.wordpress.com/2014/06/08/911-icts-passenger-lists-and-mohamad-attas-miraculous-passport/

[57] *Terror on the Tube*, p. 83-84.

[58] http://www.telegraph.co.uk/news/2016/03/24/brussels-attacks-airport-bombers-suicide-note-to-his-mother/

[59] "Liquid Lies: The Transportation Security Administration is Political, Not Practical," http://fee.org/articles/liquid-lies/ debunks the binary liquid airline bomb myth, and *Terror on the Tube* debunks home-made TATP generally and for use on board trains.

[60] http://www.businessinsider.com/isis-car-bombs-destroyed-everything-2015-7

an army of mercenaries with a dash of Salafi jargon for camouflage. Everyone has to make a living, and that is the main reason most men join the army. I am putting my money on money as the motive; either they were hired into a police sting, or it was another crime job, paymaster unknown. One more conjecture: did the explosions occur at the airport and the train station because the hunted men were promised an escape from the trap?

Najim Laachraoui, with the luggage cart next to Bakraoui in the CCTV image, was accused of making the Paris 11/13/15 suicide belts, based on "DNA traces" on them — yet they were not sure whether he was blown up at Brussels airport or not, and they do not even seem to have solid evidence there was a suicide bomber on the metro train in Maelbeek station. Laachraoui spent time in Syria, but his family noticed no change or radicalization in him on his return. He is described as a very nice and intelligent young man, as were the four "Lads from Leeds," the London patsies. Is the propaganda objective to cast jihadism as mysteriously powerful and all Muslims as inherently dangerous, when even nice fellows with a future can suddenly and unexpectedly do the most awful things?

Salah Abdeslam's brother claims that he decided not to explode his suicide vest in Paris in order to "save lives." Was he surprised when the drill went live?

• **Drills** are always something to look for in false flag or state sponsored terror events. In this case there are not the usual signs, but they might not have been needed, or the accused terrorists might have been doing drills that went live. Plus drills are getting to be too well-known. However, three weeks earlier, on 2/29/16, there was "the biggest disaster training exercise ever seen in Europe."[61] The date is interesting — Leap Year's Day, the 29th, or 2+9=11, with the month and year of 2/16 adding up to 9 — another 9/11.

• **Crisis actors.**

Perhaps the most bizarre and extremely questionable story to come out since the Brussels attacks, were the reports of Mason Wells, a Mormon missionary, who allegedly survived three separate terror attacks since 2013 – Boston, Paris and Brussels.

Back in 2013, just after the Boston marathon bombing, the Washington Post ran an article including some interesting statistics

---

[61] http://www.telegraph.co.uk/news/uknews/terrorism-in-the-uk/12177367/Tower-block-collapses-into-underground-station-in-Europes-biggest-disaster-training-exercise.html

about terror directly from the National Counterterrorism Center, which stated that:

In the last five years, the odds of an American being killed in a terrorist attack have been about 1 in 20 million.

Just another coincidence? At those odds, it's a near impossibility, and more likely we are looking at a role player of sorts.[62]

The game being played could be to enhance the normal, emotional-subjective misjudgment that the odds of being targeted by terrorism are much higher, and that terrorist attacks are much more frequent, than they really are.

Various commentators have also noted strong Mormon links to the CIA, MI6 or Mossad.

• Police state laws and reprisals are ready to go.

An infamous example is the so-called Patriot Act, 363 pages that Congress never had time to read, but "was already written and ready to go long before September 11th."[63] A "former top adviser to Hillary Clinton started calling for a Syrian invasion within just hours of the attacks."[64] The August 2013 chemicals weapons false flag in Ghouta, Syria nearly triggered massive US airstrikes on Syria.

Paul Craig Roberts again:

The attacks blamed on Muslim terrorists fit every agenda that is out there. Government agendas for more war, military spending, and police state measures are served. But so also are the agendas of those who want to limit immigration, those who want to blame the bombings on blowback from Western imperialism, those such as the Russian government who desire a united front against terrorism, and those who use the bombings to stress the innate goodness of the West, which attracts hatred because of its goodness. Washington likes the bombings because they keep Europeans scared and the governments under Washington's thumb.

Anyone who raises real questions is set upon by every group for whom the bombings blamed on ISIS are a blessing to their agenda.[65]

---

[62] http://www.globalresearch.ca/brussels-terror-attacks-masterminds-fake-cctv-footage-eu-funded-terror-drills-prior-knowledge/5516703

[63] http://www.globalissues.org/article/342/the-usa-patriot-act-was-planned-before-911

[64] http://theeconomiccollapseblog.com/archives/tag/strange-questions

[65] http://www.paulcraigroberts.org/2016/03/25/is-the-latest-isis-attack-another-false-flag-paul-craig-roberts/

To each his own propaganda. Israel has its agenda of proxy wars on its neighbors, Erdogan wants anti-Kurdish propaganda for domestic consumption, ISIS needs propaganda to boast about. ISIS purportedly claimed the bombings through social media and twitter, although hackers have traced its IP addresses to UK government agencies...[66]

Roberts appended this comment from a reader to his article:

> Let me report a bizarre thing from Poland. One, the right-wing PM immediately declared that there will be no refugees accepted in Poland, and it seems the authorities were waiting for such an event. Two, it came out the right-wing government... forced a draft of an extreme anti-terrorism bill, which grants virtually unlimited power to the secret police... It also grants the secret police access to all IT systems within Poland, and, most oddly, forces the registration of pre-paid telephone SIM cards, which were always accessible in Poland for a fee of just 5 PLN (ca. US$1.25) at any kiosk, supermarket or gas station without any need to provide your ID and/or address.

The attacks are used by opponents to letting in refugees, although the accused were not even refugees, they are native Belgian citizens. Similarly, 9/11 was used to renew the wars on Iraq, although it was impossible to link Iraq to the attacks, and the alleged hijackers were Saudis.

• Broad hints and winks take the place of proofs.

What solid evidence is there for the official story line? As with all the false flags in the "war on terror," the media present a cinematic collage that makes quite an impression, but is not based on any logical proof. There is no way of knowing if the exhibits and allegations are fabricated, but on past experience, we should assume they are. The first videos shown by the media turned out to be of an airport bombing in Moscow in 2011. One critic says the CCTV photo supposedly showing the bombers with their luggage carts in the airport was released too soon to be authentic.[67]

Logically, if the bombings were independently planned and directed from a jihadist terror central in the ISIS capital of Raqqa, as Ha'aretz claims, then where would all the claptrap of a Gladio-9/11 type false flag come from?

---

[66] http://www.zerohedge.com/news/2015-12-15/isis-twitter-handles-traced-uk-government-hackers
[67] http://www.globalresearch.ca/the-brussels-attacks-what-is-true-what-is-fake-three-daesh-suspects-at-brussels-airport/5516269

ISIS itself, as shown in the body of this book, is not an independent entity. It is financed and run by US proxies Saudi Arabia and Turkey. Erdogan, his son Bilal, and his secret service MIT are intimately involved in its operations. ISIS has no capability to independently mount an attack in the West without being infiltrated, to say the least; more to the point, ISIS itself has been created, and not just infiltrated, by the West.

The most likely scenario is that the plot was organized by NATO/Gladio (HQ in Brussels), NATO member Turkey (Erdogan and Turkish Gladio), *possibly* ISIS representatives during the patsies' visit to Turkey, and Israel (ICTS). The accused were petty criminals recruited for pay. What role they were to play is conjecture, but they didn't plan to be killed, as they had no suicide motive: not one single sign has been given that they were fundamentalists. But they were bold: they were bank robbers.

Most ISIS "jihadis" are mercenaries. Saudi Arabia emptied its jails to send its felons via Turkey to hack up Syria. As for faith-based warfare, even the few religious fanatics might not be quite as crazy as they are made out to be. Perhaps they are motivated to fight for their grand caliphate in the Muslim lands, but aren't lured by getting killed to blow up their neighbors in Europe for no reason?

(Fun Fact: This essay has 5411 words, 119 paragraphs, and 499 lines.)

— John-Paul Leonard,
San Diego, Calif.
4/4/16

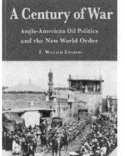

Gods of Money: Wall Street and the Death of the American Century. The banksters stop at nothing: setting world wars, plunging our world in chaos and corruption. 390 pp, $24.95.

Seeds of Destruction: The Hidden Agenda of Genetic Manipulation. A corporate gang is out for complete control of the world by patenting our food. Inside the corporate boardrooms and science labs, a world of greed, intrigue, corruption and coercion. 340 pp, $25.95.

Target China: How Washington and Wall Street Plan to Cage the Asian Dragon. The secret war on many fronts to thwart the Chinese challenge. 256 pp, $24.95.

Three by Michel Chossudovsky

Towards a World War III Scenario: The Dangers of Nuclear War. The Pentagon is preparing a first-strike nuclear attack on Iran. 103 pp, $15.95.

The Global Economic Crisis: The Great Depression of the XXI Century, by Prof. Chossudovsky, with a dozen other experts. 416 pp, $25.95.

The Globalization of Poverty and the New World Order. Brilliant analysis how corporatism feeds on poverty, destroying the environment, apartheid, racism, sexism, and ethnic strife. 401 pp, $27.95.

Two by Henry Makow

Illuminati: Cult that Hijacked the World tackles taboos like Zionism, British Empire, Holocaust. How international bankers stole a monopoly on government credit, and took over the world. They run it all: wars, schools, media. 249 pp, $19.95. ***Illuminati 2: Deception & Seduction***, more hidden history. 285 pp, $19.95

History

Two by George Seldes, the great muckraking journalist, whistleblower on the plutocrats who keep the media in lockstep, and finance fascism. ***1,000 Americans Who Rule the USA*** (1947, 324 pp, $18.95) Media concentration is nothing new! ***Facts and Fascism*** (1943, 292 pp, $15.95) How our native corporatist élite aimed for a fascist victory in WW2.

Two by Prof. Donald Gibson. ***Battling Wall Street: The Kennedy Presidency***. JFK: a martyr who strove mightily for social and economic justice. 208 pp, $14.95. ***The Kennedy Assassination Cover-Up***. JFK was murdered by the moneyed elite, not the CIA or Mafia. 375 pp, $19.95.

Two by Stewart H. Ross. ***Global Predator: US Wars for Empire***. A damning account of the atrocities committed by US armed forces over two centuries. ***Propaganda for War: How the US was Conditioned to Fight the Great War*** Propaganda by Britain and her agents like Teddy Roosevelt sucked the USA into the war to smash the old world order. 350 pp and $18.95 each.

Fall of the Arab Spring: from Revolution to Destruction. Protests as cover for destabilization. 205 pp, $14.95.

Enemies by Design: Inventing the War on Terrorism. A century of imperialism in the Middle East. Biography of Osama bin Ladeen; Zionization of America; PNAC, Afghanistan, Palestine, Iraq. 416 pp, $17.95.

The Iraq Lie: How the White House Sold the War, by former Congressman Joseph M. Hoeffel. Bush Lied about WMD — and went ahead with war. $14.95

The Nazi Hydra in America: Suppressed History of a Century by Glen Yeadon. US plutocrats launched Hitler, then recouped Nazi assets to erect today's police state. Fascists won WWII because they ran both sides. "The story is shocking and sobering, and deserves to be widely read." – Howard Zinn. 700 pp, $19.95.

Inside the Gestapo: Hitler's Shadow over the World. Intimate, fascinating Nazi defector's tale of ruthlessness, intrigue, and geopolitics. 287 pp, $17.95.

Sunk: The Story of the Japanese Submarine Fleet, 1941-1945. The bravery of doomed men in a lost cause, against impossible odds. 300 pp, $15.95.

Terrorism and the Illuminati, A 3000-Year History. "Islamic" terrorists are tentacles of western imperialism. 332 pp, $16.95.

Troublesome Country. Throughout its history the US has failed to live up to our guiding democratic creed. 146 pp, $12.95.

Psychology: Brainwashing

The Rape of the Mind: The Psychology of Thought Control, Menticide and Brainwashing. Conditioning in open and closed societies; tools to defend against torture or social pressure. Classic by Dr Joost Meerloo, survivor of Nazism and McCarthyism. 320 pp, $16.95.

The Telescreen: An Empirical Study of the Destruction of Consciousness, by Prof. Jeffrey Grupp. How mass media brainwash us with consumerism and war propaganda. Fake history, news, issues, and reality steal our souls. 199 pp, $14.95. Also by Grupp: ***Telemention: Cosmic Feeling and the Law of Attraction.*** Deep feeling is our secret nature and key to self-realization. 124 pp, $12.95.

Conspiracy, NWO

Corporatism: the Secret Government of the New World Order by Prof. Jeffrey Grupp. Corporations control all world resources. Their New World Order is the "prison planet" that Hitler aimed for. 408 pp, $16.95.

Descent into Slavery. How the banksters took over America and the world. The Founding Fathers, Rothschilds, the Crown and the City, world wars, globalization. 310 pp, $16. Also by Des Griffin: *Fourth Reich of the Rich*, 316 pp, $16.

Dope Inc.: Britain's Opium War against the United States. "The Book that Drove Kissinger Crazy." Underground Classic, new edition. 320 pp, $12.95.

Ecology, Ideology and Power by Prof. Donald Gibson. Ulterior motives of the reactionary elite pushing population and resource control. 162 pp., $14.95

Final Warning: A History of the New World Order by D. A. Rivera. Classic, in-depth research into the Great Conspiracy: the Fed, the Trilateral Commission, the CFR, and the Illuminati. 360 pp, $14.95.

How the World Really Works by A.B. Jones. Crash course in conspiracy. Digests of 11 classics like *Tragedy and Hope, Creature from Jekyll Island*. 336 pp, $15.

Killing us Softly: the Global Depopulation Policy by Kevin Galalae, 146 pp., color. The Why and How of the covert, indirect war on the people. $15.95.

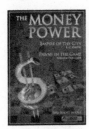

The Money Power: Empire of the City and Pawns in the Game. Two classic geopolitics books in one. The illuminist Three World Wars conspiracy: to divide us on ethnic and political lines to conquer humanity. 320 pp, $16.95

The Triumph of Consciousness. The real Global Warming and Greening agenda: more hegemony by the NWO. 347 pp, $14.95.

Conspiracy: False Flag Operations

9/11 on Trial: The W T C Collapse. 20 proofs the World Trade Center was destroyed by controlled demolition. 192 pp, $12.95.

Conspiracies, Conspiracy Theories and the Secrets of 9/11, German bestseller explores conspiracy in history, before tackling competing theories on 9/11. 274 pp, $14.95.

Author Biographies

"George Washington" – the pen name for the head writer at Washington's Blog – is a busy professional, a former adjunct professor, an American and a family man. He is post-partisan ... believing that neither the Republican nor Democratic parties represent the interests of the people as opposed to the big banks, major corporations, and the military-industrial complex. He strives to provide real-time, well-researched and actionable information.

Wayne Madsen is an American journalist, television news commentator, online editor of Wayne Madsen Report.com, investigative journalist and author specializing in intelligence and international affairs. Throughout Wayne's career he has uncovered many explosive stories, reporting from places like Washington, Iraq, Israel, the Congo, Rwanda, Pakistan, Hong Kong, Libya, Thailand, Cambodia, London, Paris, Venezuela. He has interviewed famous people and heads of state. Wayne has written for many daily, weekly, and monthly publications, and has been a television commentator on many programs, including *60 Minutes, Russia Today, Press TV*. He has authored ten books.

Made in the USA
Coppell, TX
17 June 2023

18225345R00090